Waterfalls

OF THE SMOKIES

Waterfalls

OF THE SMOKIES

Text by
Hal Hubbs, Charles Maynard, & David Morris

GREAT SMOKY MOUNTAINS ASSOCIATION

© 1992, 2002, 2006 Great Smoky Mountains Association. All rights
reserved. Published 1992. Second Edition 2006.

Edited by Kent Cave and Steve Kemp

Design Format by Christina Watkins

Production by Shelly Powell, Amy Campbell, and Lisa Horstman

Cartography by University of Tennessee Cartography

Printed in China

1 2 3 4 5 6 7 8 9

ISBN 0-937207-51-9

Great Smoky Mountains Association is a nonprofit organization which
supports the educational, scientific, and historical programs of Great
Smoky Mountains National Park. Our publications are an educational
service intended to enhance the public's understanding and enjoyment
of the national park. If you would like to know more about our publications, memberships, and projects, please contact:
Great Smoky Mountains Association, 115 Park Headquarters Road,
Gatlinburg, TN 37738 (865) 436-7318.   www.SmokiesStore.org

This book is for Elizabeth, Janice, and Carol
who share our lives and our love of the mountains.

ACKNOWLEDGMENTS

We are grateful for the assistance of many who helped us prepare this book. Our children, Brian, Caroline, Anna, Ben, John, and Will helped us measure and photograph many falls. Glenn Cardwell, former Supervisory Park Ranger at Sugarlands; Annette Hartigan, Park Librarian; Kitty Manscill, former Museum Curator; Gene Cox, former Chief of Visitor Services; Eldon Wanrow, former Supervisory Park Ranger at Cades Cove; Kent Cave, Staff Park Ranger; George Minnigh, Backcountry Specialist; Steve Kemp, Interpretive Products and Services Director; and Donna Lane, former GSMA Sales Coordinator at Sugarlands, were all most helpful with information and suggestions. Julie Brown, Carolyn Jourdan, Elizabeth Hubbs, Carol Morris, Janice Maynard, Marianne Wightman, and Nancy Best proofread and edited. Special thanks to Bob "The Wheel" Lochbaum for distance measurements.

CONTENTS

Map of Great Smoky Mountains National Park *10*
Introduction *12*
Timeless Waters *14*

BIG CREEK

Gunter Fork Cascades *21*
Midnight Hole *27*
Mouse Creek Falls *30*

CADES COVE–TOWNSEND

Abrams Falls *35*
Crooked Arm Cascade *40*
Indian Flats Falls *43*
Laurel Creek Cascade *48*
Lynn Camp Prong Cascades *51*
Spruce Flats Falls *54*
White Oak Flats Cascades *59*

CHEROKEE–DEEP CREEK

Chasteen Creek Cascade............. *67*
Flat Creek Falls *69*
Indian Creek Falls *72*
Juney Whank Falls *75*
Little Creek Falls *79*
Mingo Falls *83*
Sweat Heifer Cascades *87*

Three Waterfalls Loop 92
Tom Branch Falls 95

CLINGMANS DOME
Forney Creek Cascade 100
Road Prong Cascade 105
Road Prong Falls 109

COSBY
Hen Wallow Falls 115
Noisy Creek Cascades 119

FONTANA
Hazel Creek Cascades 124
Twentymile Cascade 131

GATLINBURG–MT. LE CONTE
Baskins Creek Falls 137
Cataract Falls 143
Fern Branch Falls 145
Grotto Falls 149
Huskey Branch Falls 153
Jakes Creek Falls 159
Laurel Falls 161
Mannis Branch Falls 165
Meigs Falls 169
Place of a Thousand Drips 172
Rainbow Falls 175

Ramsey Cascades *181*
The Sinks *185*
Twin Falls *187*
Upper Meigs Falls *192*

Tips for Waterfall Photography *197*
Resources *200*
Index *202*
Photography Credits *205*

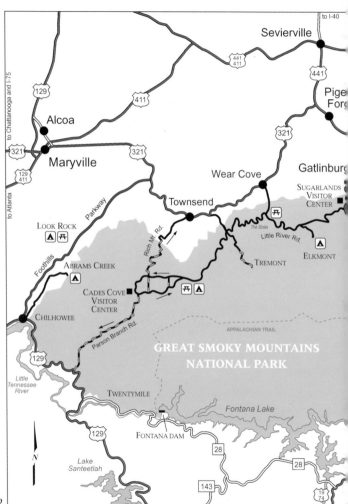

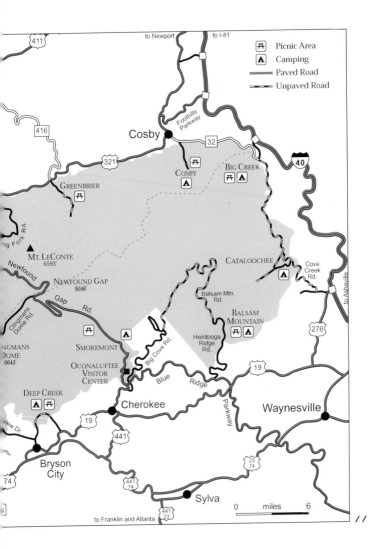

INTRODUCTION

*W*aterfalls and cascades cannot be adequately captured in words or photographs. They must be seen, experienced. This book attempts to point out interesting features and the location of over forty falls and cascades in Great Smoky Mountains National Park. Not all of the falls in the park are included. This book calls attention to some of the more spectacular or accessible falls and cascades of the Smokies.

For purposes of clarity, the terms "waterfall" and "cascade" designate two types of phenomena. "Waterfall" is water in a vertical or free fall over a cliff. Only a few falls actually free fall away from a rocky face. Rainbow and Grotto Falls are two of the primary examples. "Cascade" is used to describe water as it rushes down rocks and rocky ledges. Ramsey Cascade and Laurel Falls are good examples of this. However, the lines are blurred in many instances. Gunter Fork and Juney Whank Falls can fit both categories. It's a challenge to describe the elusive, liquid nature of falls and cascades.

Measuring the falls presents another challenge. Where does a cascade begin or end? Is a steep cascade above or below a falls included? Is a cascade measured by its fall in elevation or by the distance it travels? All these questions and more present themselves to observers of creeks and streams of the park.

For cascades, both the fall or drop in elevation as well as the distance the water travels over the rocks are provided. Gunter Fork falls 100 feet and travels 285 feet. Huskey Branch travels 120 feet but only falls about 50 feet. For free falling water, the distance the water falls from cliff top to rocky base or plunge pool is measured.

Measurements were made with a plumb line and altimeter to give the best guesses on the height and distance of the falls. The descriptions of the falls include directional notes (right and left). The orientation is always as if the observer is facing the falls.

When planning to see a waterfall, bear in mind that rainfall has a direct effect on how much water will be in the stream. September and October are the driest months while July is one of the wettest. It is disappointing to find only a trickle when a falls is expected. The precipitation is greater for the higher elevations. Waterflow is dependent on the total area drained by the creek as well as rainfall.

As beautiful as waterfalls and cascades are, they can be most dangerous. Stay on established and maintained trails. These have been constructed for your safety. Observe all warning signs. Use common sense. Wet, moss-covered rocks are slippery. Ice coats the rocks beside streams and falls in the winter. Many fatalities and innumerable injuries have occurred when people have attempted to climb to the tops of waterfalls. Keep in mind that medical assistance in the backcountry is several hours away.

The terrain of the park and its annual rainfall of over 85 inches make for an abundance of falls and cascades. Enjoy these beautiful and magical features of Great Smoky Mountains National Park.

TIMELESS WATERS

*B*eside Grotto Falls only the sound of Roaring Fork can be heard. The water falling off the overhanging ledge of sandstone fills the air with mist. All other sounds of the forest are blocked out and even conversation becomes impossible. A friend and I yelled at each other simply to be heard. No birds, no rush of wind through the leaves, no hammering of woodpeckers, nor swish of leaves underfoot. Nothing but the sound of water.

Upon listening carefully I discovered that the falls have two distinct sounds. One is a SSSHHH sound of drops leaving the cliff and falling through the air. The other sound is the splash and roar of water striking the rocks and pool below. This sound overpowers all noise. Stand at the foot of Grotto, Rainbow, Laurel, any falls. Let the sounds silence you long enough to hear the story of the mountains, a story best told at the waterfalls.

The rock walls, the jumble of smooth stones tell the story of forces that formed the mountains. Water and gravity shape the Great Smoky Mountains. When the two combine to make waterfalls and cascades, the results are fascinating and beautiful as well as formative. Due to annual precipitation nearly equal to that of a rain forest and rugged topography, waterfalls and cascades abound along the 2,100 miles of streams in the Great Smoky Mountains.

The Smokies were and are carved by water. Water has shaped the mountains and valleys into their present form. Stand on a peak to look down on the jumble of mountains, ridges, valleys and ravines. Look carefully. Notice the slopes, the peaks, the twinkle of sunlight on water. Water sculpted this marvelous landscape.

At waterfalls this creative action is most dramatic. A torrent pours over cliff or bare rock face to plunge into a deep pool. Large logs against the escarpment, smooth boulders and pebbles are evidence of the power of water to move, to shape, to carve the terrain.

Water isn't the only tool that built the mountains. Over 240 million years ago the earth's crust shifted in ways that pushed up an enormous mountain range higher than today's Rockies. The rocks that were exposed as they were forced upward had been formed 545 million to 800 million years before. The original mountains were worn down by the erosive action of water until only a plain was left. More warping of the surface due to crustal movements caused the plain to rise above sea level. Water continued to cut through this plain.

Today's Smokies are actually a result of the water erosion cutting through the primal plain. The landscape has been described as one of "valleys cut between ridges rather than that of ridges rising between valleys." However, it's not the water that does the wearing, the cutting. Logs, rocks, grains of sand all borne by the streams wear away the mountains. It could be said that water assists the mountains to break down themselves.

From where does this water come? The Smokies receive over 85 inches of precipitation each year in the highest elevations. Of that precipitation over 40% evaporates or is used by plants. Water in the air is one reason the mountains are "smoky." The mist of the mountains often obscures the terrain that is being worn away.

In addition to the land, waterfalls break down light itself. Sunlight is shattered into colored frequencies as it passes through the refracting mist of falling water. The sunlight sifting through the trees strikes Rainbow Falls, Ramsey Cascades, or Abrams Falls only to be broken into colors. Just as the strata of rock are revealed at the falls, the strata of light are seen in the rainbows and double rainbows of the falls.

Loren Eisley wrote, "If there is magic on this planet, it is contained in water." Water certainly contains some of the magic of the mountains. The streams brim with life. The thick stands of rhododendron, ferns and wildflowers crowd creek banks as evidences of the magical force. Deer, bear, snakes, otters, wolves, crayfish and salamanders are only a few of the myriad animals that drink from or live in the water that rushes down the mountains.

The Cherokee, native Americans who lived in the area before the settlers came, said the waters of the mountains were inhabited by the Nunne'hi, the water spirits. The Cherokee built villages beside the swift currents of mountain rivers. European settlers followed this example in building their own dwellings and farms. They put the fall of water to use with mills which ground grain into meal and sawed timber into lumber to sustain and shelter life.

Humans have endangered the miracle of the mountain

waters over the years. Logging stripped the mountains of vegetation and took a toll in the streams. Native brook trout were
choked in the silt-filled waters. Animals were unable to live in
the open, logged areas. Water's force was magnified since
fewer roots were unable to check its power. With the creation
of the national park, logging ceased and the mountains began
to regenerate. Life's return to the naked chines was a magic
assisted through the abundance of water.

Former inhabitants of the Smokies once returned to visit
cemeteries and to drink from mountain springs. Although it's
now unsafe to drink from the streams, those settlers once said,
"Mountain water is healthier. It'll make yore days longer."
Some drank the water's magic to live longer, remember better.

Stories are told of an earlier time when houses were built not
for the view but for the availability of water. Today rotting logs
and foundation stones lie beside creeks as a reminder of another
day's dependence on the mountain's plentiful supply of water.

Waterfalls concentrate the magic of water into a sensory
experience. The wetness of the mist cools hot skin. The crisp taste
refreshes the weary traveler while the smell of thick vegetation
speaks of life. Watching the falling water induces a trance which
pushes aside all concerns. The sound, the double sound of a
waterfall, overpowers until nothing else but the falls can be
heard, seen, tasted, smelled, felt. Then the mountains can be
experienced. Stand at Grotto, at Rainbow, at Laurel, at Abrams,
at any of the myriad falls and cascades in the Smokies. Experience the miracle of this planet in the fall of water.　　—CWM

Waterfalls

OF THE SMOKIES

BIG CREEK

BIG CREEK

Big Creek is one of the most scenic creeks in the entire park. From the Walnut Bottom area to its junction with the Pigeon River, Big Creek drops about 1,200 feet (120 stories), or an average of 200 feet per mile. The change in elevation causes many beautiful cascades and small falls on this large creek. The trail stays close to the creek so that its sights and sounds can be fully enjoyed. The cascades and falls that are on Big Creek and its tributaries are some of the most beautiful in the Great Smoky Mountains.

The Big Creek basin was logged by the Crestmont Lumber Company in the early 1900s. Many of the trails follow old logging railroad beds. Evidence of the logging days can be found—steel cables, rails, spikes, old road beds. The forest, mostly hardwoods and spruce-fir, has recovered well from being logged.

To reach Big Creek, take the Waterville Exit (#451) on I-40 about 60 miles east of Knoxville or 50 miles west of Asheville. Cross the Pigeon River and turn left at the end of the bridge over which the Appalachian Trail crosses. Follow the road past the Waterville Power Plant to an intersection two miles from the interstate. Continue straight through the intersection up a narrow road to the ranger station. The picnic area and campground are beyond the ranger station about 0.8 mile.

This area is popular due to its closeness to the interstate and its wilderness setting. The falls and cascades are without equal.

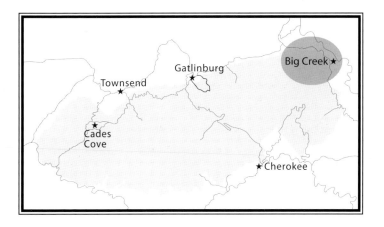

GUNTER FORK CASCADES

- **2 CASCADES**
- **30 FOOT DROP**
- **100 FOOT DROP, 285 FOOT RUN**
- **16.3 MILE ROUNDTRIP STRENUOUS HIKE**

*G*unter Fork is a major tributary of Big Creek. Named after a family that settled in the mountains of Cocke County, Tennessee and Haywood County, North Carolina, Gunter Fork originates on the northeastern flank of Balsam Mountain between Luftee Knob and Big Cataloochee Mountain.

Gunter Fork Cascades

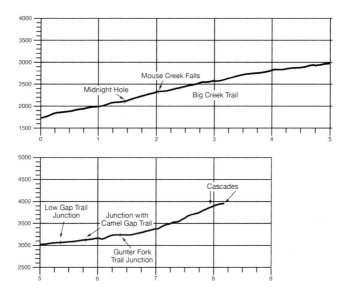

The first cascade/falls is on the right about 1.8 miles up the Gunter Fork Trail. Gunter Fork splits into two streams as it pours over the exposed sandstone which is inclined from left to right at about 60°. The left stream takes a higher route ending in a 10 foot falls, while the right stream slides down the quartz-streaked sandstone at a 45° slant. The water ends in a sizeable plunge pool after falling a total of 30 feet.

Look around the falls. A small cascade tumbles down the steep rock face 40 feet to the right of the falls. In dry weather

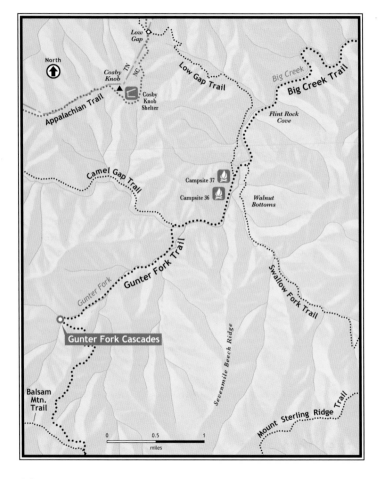

this small cascade disappears. In wet seasons it puts on a show which rivals the main attraction. Steel cable above the falls is a leftover from earlier logging days.

Only 0.3 mile beyond this cascade is one of the most dramatic falls of water in the park. In a drop of 100 feet in elevation the water of Gunter Fork cascades a distance of 285 feet. It begins as a shallow cascade of 40 feet down an easy slope of 20°. The water then plunges 25 feet straight down in a dazzling falls. From the base of the falls it is 220 feet to a small, shallow pool beside which the trail passes.

The creek is 15 feet wide at the top. After the falls the stream widens as it spreads over an exposed surface of Thunderhead Sandstone which displays many interesting qualities. Near the base of the cascade the rock changes from a knobby conglomerate which resembles cobblestone to a smooth, fine-grained sandstone. The line between these two rock types is well defined, running up from left to right at a 40° angle.

The face of the cascades is sloped like the roof of a house. Do not climb because it can be very dangerous due to wet rocks or ice. The whole scene can be enjoyed from the base where one can listen to the symphony of sounds made by the water and forest. More steel cable ties the present to the logging past.

Though far from the roads, they are well worth the effort. The upper cascade is one of the tallest in the Smokies.

TO GET THERE: The hike to Gunter Fork Cascades begins from

Big Creek Picnic Area (see directions at the beginning of this chapter). Walk up the Big Creek Trail 5.8 miles past Midnight Hole, Mouse Creek Falls, Brakeshoe Springs, and Walnut Bottoms. After the Walnut Bottoms backcountry campsites, the Gunter Fork Trail begins at mile 6.4.

At the beginning of the Gunter Fork Trail, Big Creek must be crossed. Except in the driest seasons this is usually a wet crossing. Be careful on the slippery rocks. With high water, the stream may be impassable. Once the crossing of Big Creek is out of the way, Gunter Fork or its tributaries are crossed eight times. This can be done with careful rock hopping.

The first cascade mentioned is 7.9 miles from the Big Creek trailhead (1.8 miles from the beginning of the Gunter Fork Trail). The tall upper cascade is 0.3 mile beyond, bringing the entire walk to 8.2 miles. A scenic view of the Gunter Fork-Big Creek valley is 0.3 mile beyond the upper cascade in a small heath bald. The hike to the upper cascade on Gunter Fork is a long 16.3 mile roundtrip day hike. It's fun to camp in the Walnut Bottom backcountry site, which requires a reservation through the Backcountry Office. The campsite is a very popular one, but enjoyable under the hemlocks beside Big Creek.

The effort that is spent in reaching the upper cascade is well rewarded not just with one of the highest falls in the park, but with many scenic falls on the trek up.

MIDNIGHT HOLE

- **DOUBLE FALLS**
- **8 FOOT DROP**
- **2.8 MILE ROUNDTRIP EASY HIKE**

*M*idnight Hole is well named. A huge pool over 80 feet across and 15 feet deep is filled with the clear water of Big Creek. The pool is a dark green in winter and dark as midnight in the summer. Enormous boulders squeeze Big Creek to a small 15 foot opening through which two falls of 8 feet pour. The stream on the right is the stronger of the two. In wet weather, water spills over the rock that divides the two to form a single falls. The beauty of the setting more than makes up for what the falls lack in height.

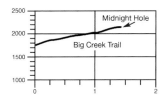

The fine-grained gray boulders are Thunderhead Sandstone. They provide wonderful places for picnics or spots to fish. Fishermen love the area for the easily located trout that populate the clear waters of Big Creek. An iron rail beside Midnight Hole is a reminder of the logging days at the turn of the century. Midnight Hole is an extra special place in a gorgeous valley.

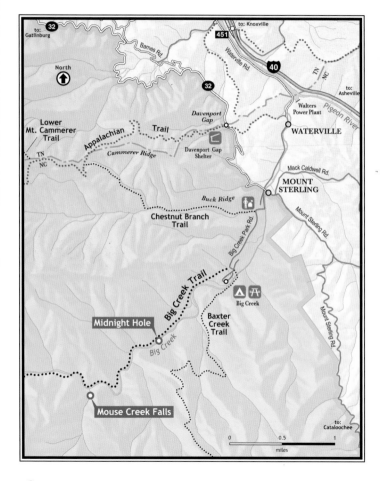

Midnight Hole

TO GET THERE: The hike to Midnight Hole begins from Big Creek Picnic Area (see directions at the beginning of this chapter). Walk up Big Creek Trail 1.4 miles. Midnight Hole is on the left. Horse hitches are available. The walk is on an old jeep road that is wide and gently graded so that even the inexperienced hiker can make it. With a little more time it's only 0.6 mile further to Mouse Creek Falls.

MOUSE CREEK FALLS

- **CASCADE**
- **50 FOOT DROP**
- **4 MILE ROUNDTRIP MODERATE HIKE**

*M*ouse Creek Falls is a beautiful hourglass-shaped cascade at the mouth of Mouse Creek. Several streams intertwine to pass through a 4 foot opening before spreading again to form a wide base of falling water. A small pool at the base slows the water as it crosses an old logging railroad bed. The water then cascades another 10 feet to join Big Creek.

The headwaters of Mouse Creek are high on the slopes of Mount Sterling (5,842 feet in elevation) which has one of the few remaining fire towers in the park. A bench on the banks of Big Creek, opposite Mouse Creek Falls, provides a good place to enjoy the play of water as it bounds down the rocks. Near the top of the cascade water pours into a small hole in such a way that it leaps back into the air.

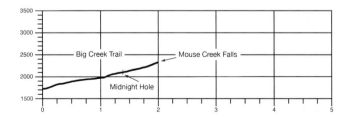

Mouse Creek Falls

TO GET THERE: The hike to Mouse Creek Falls begins from Big Creek Picnic Area (see directions at the beginning of this chapter and map on page 28). Mouse Creek Falls is 2 miles up the Big Creek Trail. This moderate walk on a wide roadbed gains 500 feet in elevation in the 2 miles. The trail is open to horses and hikers. On the way up the trail notice the change in rock as you pass over the Greenbrier Fault. The rock changes from the more stratified Rich Butt Sandstone to the more solid Thunderhead Sandstone. Also, stop at Midnight Hole at 1.4 miles.

Waterfalls
OF THE SMOKIES
CADES COVE–TOWNSEND

CADES COVE–TOWNSEND

Cades Cove is a picturesque mountain valley in the western part of the park. Its popularity is due to outstanding scenery and plentiful wildlife. The 11 mile loop is a popular auto trail, especially in the fall. The Cades Cove Visitor Center at the Cable Mill Historic Area is half way around the one-way loop.

Townsend, once a logging center, is a small town at the western entrance to Great Smoky Mountains National Park. Townsend can be reached via Highway 321 20 miles southeast of Maryville and 15 miles southwest of Pigeon Forge. From Gatlinburg take Highway 73 (Little River Road) 18 miles to the "Y", which is an intersection of roads and rivers that is very popular. It's only 7 more miles from the "Y" to Cades Cove.

The two-way Laurel Creek Road is the only entrance into Cades Cove. Two additional exits leaving the cove are both one-way gravel roads. Rich Mountain Road goes over Rich Mountain to Townsend and Parson Branch Road traverses Hannah Mountain to Highway 129 at Chilhowee Lake. Both are closed in winter.

Parson Branch Road follows and crosses Parson Branch. The road reaches its highest point at Sams Gap after which it descends beside Parson Branch with numerous fords to splash through. Just remember it's a long way back to Maryville or the park via the Foothills Parkway.

Rich Mountain Road, a drier route with a couple of scenic overlooks, traverses Rich Mountain into Tuckaleechee Cove and Townsend. Allow plenty of time for both roads. On days when Cades Cove is jammed with traffic, Rich Mountain and Parson

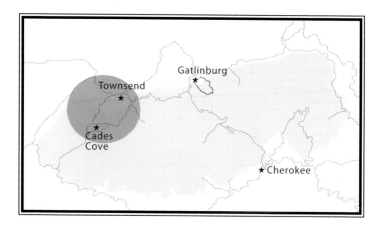

Branch afford welcome escapes.

Many falls are in the Cades Cove–Townsend area, from the scenic Spruce Flats Falls at Tremont to the popular Abrams Falls in Cades Cove.

ABRAMS FALLS

- **FALLS**
- **25 FOOT DROP**
- **5 MILE ROUNDTRIP MODERATE HIKE**

*T*he 25 foot high Abrams Falls plunges into a large pool with the volume of a small river rather than a

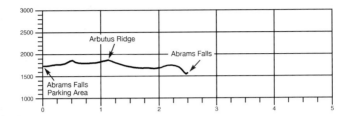

creek. Eighteen creeks and branches flow into Cades Cove to form Abrams Creek, which is the only water exit from the cove to the Little Tennessee River. The creek is 35 feet wide at the top of the falls. The plunge pool is over 100 feet long and nearly the same in width. It is tempting to swim here, but don't. The deep pool near the falls has a very strong undercurrent and at least two drownings have been recorded here in the last few years. The water is very deep with a dark green color.

The force of the falls throws spray over 50 feet into rhododendron and hemlock on the bank opposite the trail. Spray forms ice on the rocks and plants in the coldest months and cools the air in the hottest. When the early morning sun comes over the ridge and hits the falls, a beautiful rainbow can be seen. One January morning we saw a double rainbow as we stood on the rocks beside the falls. The outer rainbow's colors were in opposite order to the inside one.

Smooth pebbles and large battered logs show the force of the water. The falls thunder over a multi-layered cliff of

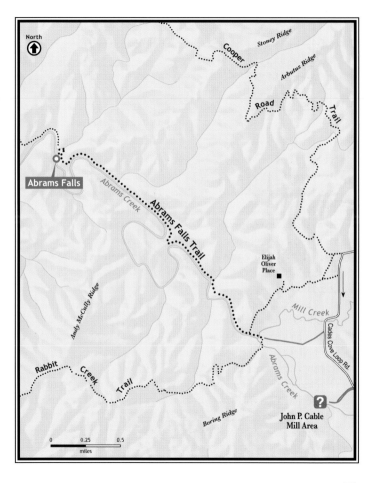

North

Stoney Ridge

Cooper

Arbutus Ridge

Road

Trail

Abrams Falls

Abrams Creek

Abrams Falls Trail

Elijah
Oliver
Place

Mill Creek

Andy McCully Ridge

Cades Cove Loop Rd.

Rabbit Creek Trail

Abrams Creek

Boring Ridge

John P. Cable
Mill Area

?

0   0.25   0.5
miles

Cades Sandstone. Above the falls are 4 or 5 1-foot steps where Abrams Creek drops over more of the sandstone which is prevalent in this area.

Abrams Creek and Falls were probably named for Old Abraham, a Cherokee who lived near the cove in Chilhowee. A Cherokee village, Tsiyahi, Otter Place, was in all likelihood named for the otters which once frolicked in the creek. River otters have been reintroduced to the Great Smoky Mountains, and Abrams Creek is one place where they are occasionally sighted.

TO GET THERE: Take Cades Cove Loop Road about 5 miles to a right turn after crossing Abrams Creek. Follow the gravel road 0.5 mile to a parking area. Start at the parking area at the junction of Mill and Abrams creeks. A footbridge crosses Abrams Creek to a trail split. To the right it's 0.5 mile through bottom land to the Elijah Oliver cabin. Straight ahead at the split is the Abrams Creek Trail, which goes through a rhododendron tunnel that is especially beautiful in early summer when it's in full bloom.

The trail generally follows the creek until it ascends a pine-covered ridge. Arbutus Branch is crossed before ascending Arbutus Ridge, 200 feet above the creek. At 1.1 miles the ridge top is gained, then the trail descends through pines and mountain laurel to a foot log over Stony Branch. A third and final ridge is climbed at 2.2 miles. A foot log across Wilson Creek is reached at 2.5 miles.

Abrams Falls

A short side trail to the left goes to the top of Abrams Falls. Use caution when at the top. Wet rocks are slippery. Continue 0.2 mile down to Wilson Creek before taking a side trail to the base of the falls.

Return to the parking lot by the same trail. This is a beauti-

ful walk in the spring and summer providing plenty of wildflowers, rhododendron and mountain laurel. This hike goes
well with a day trip to Cades Cove. Picnic at the falls or at the
Cable Mill Historic Site.

CROOKED ARM CASCADE
- **CASCADE**
- **25 FOOT DROP, 40 FOOT RUN**
- **1.4 MILE ROUNDTRIP EASY HIKE**

*T*his nice cascade can put on a wonderful show in the
wetter months but can dry to a mere trickle in drier
times. Crooked Arm Creek flows down from the sides of a
ridge by the same name to fall over a ledge of Metcalf Phyllite at the Great Smoky Mountain Fault, one of several major
geological faults that formed the mountains. Metcalf Phyllite
is a metamorphic rock which is more resistant to erosion
than the limestone which makes up the floor of Cades Cove.
Since the phyllite is multi-layered, the cascade has many
small layers that enhance the show.

Depending on the
water flow, the cas-
cades can be about 18
to 20 feet wide. It flows
down the rocky face
and then away with lit-

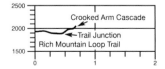

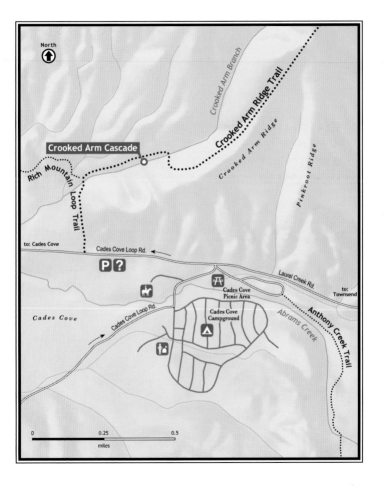

tle to no plunge pool at its base. The cascade is on the right side of the Crooked Arm Ridge Trail. The name "Crooked Arm" comes from the term "arm" which older mountain people used to refer to a ridge or spur of a mountain. This particular arm is bent like an elbow or a crooked arm.

TO GET THERE: Start at the parking area at the beginning of the 11 mile one-way Cades Cove Loop Road. The trail begins on the right side of the road near the gate to the Cades Cove Loop Road.

Crooked Arm Cascade

Walk on the Rich Mountain Loop Trail along the boundary between the woods and the fields. A fence is on the left side of the trail. After rock hopping across Crooked Arm Creek, at 0.5 mile turn right onto the Crooked Arm Ridge Trail. Follow the trail 0.2 mile to the cascade on the right. You may hear the cascade before you see it. Take the same route back to the parking area.

INDIAN FLATS FALLS
- **4 FALLS**
- **65 FOOT DROP, 170 FOOT RUN**
- **7.5 MILE ROUNDTRIP MODERATE HIKE**

*I*ndian Flats Falls is a strand of four falls whose individual beauty is magnified due to their placement on the necklace of Indian Flats Prong. When viewed from the base, Indian Flats Falls is a truly magnificent sight, but each step has a wonder of its own.

The headwaters of Indian Flats Prong are near the crest of the Smokies at Mt. Davis, Hemlock Knob, and Miry Ridge. The water, cooled by the high elevation, quickly tumbles to the falls. The trail arrives at the base of the uppermost falls which drops 20 feet in three streams into a small pool. The creek travels to the right around an island of rounded stones for 60 feet to the next ledge which is 35 feet wide.

The second step begins with the creek at a width of 10 feet, but this spreads to 16 feet when the water strikes a

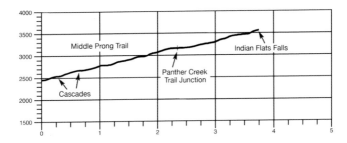

small ledge partway down the 18 foot fall. A large circular pool is at the base of the second falls. The Thunderhead Sandstone of the area is scoured clean and smooth with pockets of rounded rocks. Tilting only slightly away from the viewer, the sandstone forms the numerous ledges of the falls. The creek moves 45 more feet then drops off the third ledge. The third step is the smallest at 9 feet.

The fourth and final step is 18 feet beyond the third. The water falls 12 more feet before being squeezed back to normal creek size by boulders at the base. Round holes with pieces of quartz and other rocks resemble baskets of eggs. The rocks combine with the swirling action of the water to carve out the holes.

Thick rhododendron crowds both sides of the stream. Doghobble, trillium and hardwoods also populate the forest. Lush moss covers the rocks and ledges to form a green tapestry interwoven with bluets and trillium in the spring. Indian Flats Falls is definitely worth the trek.

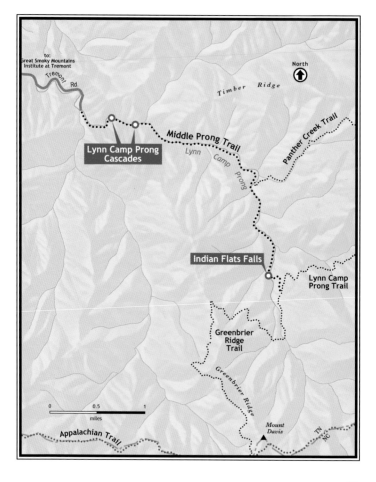

Upper step of Indian Flats Falls

TO GET THERE: From the intersection of Little River Road and Laurel Creek Road (the Townsend "Y"), go 0.2 mile toward Cades Cove (west) and turn left at the Tremont sign. Follow Tremont Road 2 miles to Great Smoky Mountains Institute. On the right, a booklet for the Tremont Logging History Auto Tour can be purchased for a small charge. Follow the gravel road 3 miles until it ends at a turnaround.

Walk the footbridge over Lynn Camp Prong to an old railroad bed which goes in two directions. Take the left fork which follows the creek along the Middle Prong Trail. Pass the cascades and falls mentioned in the Lynn Camp Prong Cascades hike. Stay on the Middle Prong Trail past the trail junction with the Panther Creek Trail. A little over 1 mile past the trail junction the trail climbs the ridge on a couple of switchbacks. Indian Flats Prong is crossed on a bridge. See the ruins of an old bridge up creek (to the right) of the present bridge.

The trail moves away from the creek and upward on more switchbacks. At the second switchback a side trail leaves the main trail on the right. Follow the side trail on an old roadbed about 150 yards to the base of the uppermost falls. The side trail isn't marked and can be overgrown in the summer. It's worth the struggle through the underbrush for this sight. Indian Flats Falls is a good day-long adventure with plenty of opportunities for viewing falls and cascades along Lynn Camp and Indian Flats Prongs.

Laurel Creek Cascade

LAUREL CREEK CASCADE

- **CASCADE**
- **8 FOOT DROP, 20 FOOT RUN**
- **ROADSIDE**

*T*his small cascade is a nice show at a parking area along one of the park's most traveled roads. Laurel Creek's headwaters are along the slopes of Crib Gap, the entrance to

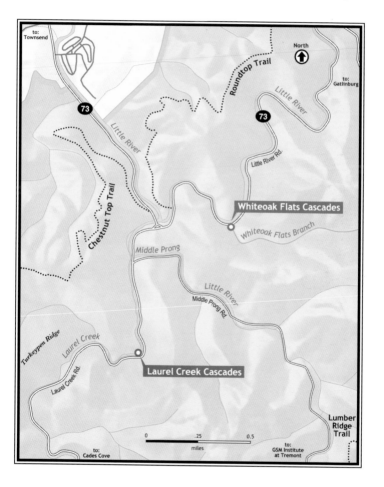

to:
Townsend

North

to:
Gatlinburg

73

Roundtop Trail

Little River

73

Little River

Little River Rd.

Whiteoak Flats Cascades

Whiteoak Flats Branch

Chestnut Top Trail

Middle Prong

Little River

Middle Prong Rd.

Turkeypen Ridge

Laurel Creek

Laurel Creek Rd.

Laurel Creek Cascades

Lumber
Ridge
Trail

0   .25   0.5
miles

to:
Cades Cove

to:
GSM Institute
at Tremont

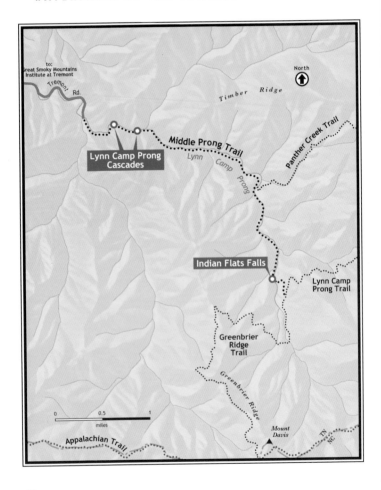

Cades Cove. The creek flows along the road to fall over this 8 foot ledge of Cades Sandstone, a gray-brown fine-grained rock. The creek slows in a large pool above the cascade. The main stream flow is to the right. Laurel Creek is a little over 30 feet wide at this point. At the base of the cascade is another plunge pool. A small unnamed creek flows in opposite from the road.

TO GET THERE: Laurel Creek Cascade is 0.4 mile west from the intersection at the Townsend "Y" on Laurel Creek Road. The small parking area between the road and the creek provides a wonderful place to get out of the flow of traffic to simply enjoy this nice creek. Very often travelers who are focused on getting to Cades Cove don't notice this beautiful little cascade.

LYNN CAMP PRONG CASCADES
- **NUMEROUS CASCADES & FALLS**
- **1.3 MILE ROUNDTRIP EASY WALK**

A sandstone cliff provides an excellent overlook of the water of Lynn Camp Prong as it rushes down a rocky chute. The creek is 10 feet wide with a good flow at the head of the upper cascade which is 35 feet long. After spreading to 20

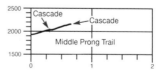

feet the water travels 85 feet to a 4 foot ledge. At the base of the cliff and the small ledge, the creek slides to the left in a small 3 foot channel for 80 feet. It then shoots down a bare rock face in a narrow stream for 55 feet where it hits a rock shelf and splashes into the air. A plunge pool at the foot catches the airborne water 10 feet after its launch.

A large gray rock face of Thunderhead Sandstone slants at about 40° making it easy to climb on. The creek is forced into a narrow confine causing it to leap into the air near the base. The drop of the falls is 65 feet from the first cascade to the plunge pool.

Sixty paces beyond the second bench is an 8 foot waterfall. Look for an old steel cable which is left from logging days. Below the small upper falls is a wonderful place to cool hot feet.

Another set of cascades is 0.25 mile up the Middle Prong Trail. Two groups of falls form these beautiful cascades. The first group is two falls of 4 and 6 feet. On the 6 foot step the stream splits into three falls. The rocks are moss-covered with rhododendron, beech and doghobble on the banks. A bench 100 feet upstream is near the upper group made up of a 2 foot and 6 foot falls.

A Civilian Conservation Corps (CCC) camp occupied an area up the road from this cascade in the early 1930s. The name Lynn Camp may come from the many Linwood (basswood) trees in the area. Or it may come from the Scotch-Irish who settled the mountains. A lin (or linn) is a small pool in a creek at the base or top of a waterfall. This creek has many a beautiful lin.

Lynn Camp Prong Cascades

TO GET THERE: From the intersection of Highway 73 (Little River Road) and Laurel Creek Road, go 0.2 mile toward Cades Cove (west) and turn left at the Tremont sign. Follow Tremont Road 2 miles to the Great Smoky Mountains Institute at Tremont. On the right a booklet for the Tremont Logging History Auto Tour can be purchased for a small charge. Follow the gravel road 3 miles until it ends at a turnaround.

Walk the footbridge over Lynn Camp Prong to an old railroad bed which goes in two directions. To the right an old railroad grade ascends 0.25 miles to a bridge. However, take the left fork which follows the creek along the Middle Prong Trail. The trail follows the route of the old logging railroad.

After 0.4 mile a bench on the left has a good view of a large cascade. Go to the second bench which overlooks the middle of the cascade. The 8 foot falls is 60 paces beyond the bench between rhododendron and a large rock. Continue 0.25 mile upstream past a rock cliff on the right of the trail and around a bend to the upper set of cascades. A bench is at the top of these.

The Middle Prong Trail changes to the Greenbrier Ridge Trail before it reaches the Appalachian Trail 7.5 miles away. This walk is fun combined with the Auto Trail and the Spruce Flats Falls Trail or as a nice side visit on the way to Cades Cove.

SPRUCE FLATS FALLS
- **4 CASCADES**
- **125 FOOT DROP, 320 FOOT RUN**
- **1.9 MILE ROUNDTRIP MODERATE HIKE**

*T*he cascades are near the confluence of Spruce Flats Branch and the Middle Prong of the Little River. The falls have been called Three Step Falls because only three can be seen from a vantage point at the base. However, a fourth

Spruce Flats Falls

cascade is 75 feet above the third one. It is beautiful as the water of Spruce Flats Creek drops 28 feet into a trough which pushes the water to the left.

The third cascade is the smallest at 17 feet. Only 20 feet separate the base of the upper cascade from the top of the middle one, which is 28 feet tall. The creek moves 100 feet before falling over the last, lowest, and largest cascade which is 60 feet tall and 60 feet wide. A large plunge pool holds the water only temporarily before it falls on down to the Middle Prong of Little River. In winter you can catch a glimpse of the falls from upper Tremont Road.

Thunderhead Sandstone, which is resistant to erosion and is streaked with quartz, makes up the cliffs at the falls. The Oconaluftee Fault runs nearby on its way to Cherokee from Cades Cove. Notice that the rocks on the left side of the falls are more rounded than the jumble of rocks on the slope to the right. The more angular stones were chipped and blasted from the cliffs to build a logging railroad bed which is about 100 feet above the lowest falls.

This area was one of the last logged by the Little River Lumber Company. Early efforts by loggers to cut timber near here were thwarted by Will Walker who, in 1859, settled the flat area where Great Smoky Mountains Institute at Tremont now stands. Walker didn't sell

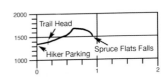

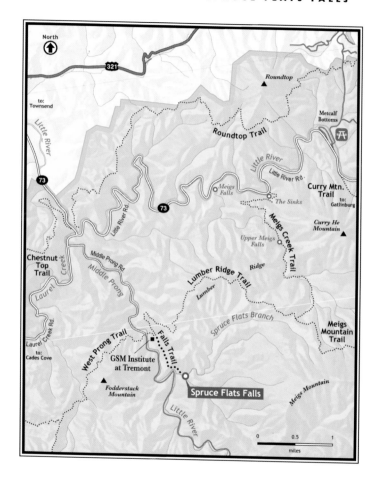

North

321

to:
Townsend

Little River

73

Roundtop Trail

Roundtop

Metcalf
Bottoms

Little River

Little River Rd.

Meigs
Falls

The Sinks

Curry Mtn.
Trail
to:
Gatlinburg

Curry He
Mountain

Chestnut
Top
Trail

Little River Rd.

73

Upper Meigs
Falls

Meigs Creek Trail

Laurel Creek

Middle Prong Rd.

Middle Prong

Lumber Ridge Trail

Ridge

Lumber

Spruce Flats Branch

Meigs
Mountain
Trail

Laurel Creek Rd.

to:
Cades Cove

West Prong Trail

Falls Trail

GSM Institute
at Tremont

Fodderstack
Mountain

Little River

Spruce Flats Falls

Meigs Mountain

0   0.5   1
miles

57

the timber rights to the area, but after his death in 1919, his heirs did.

These cascades are used for teaching at the Great Smoky Mountains Institute in its environmental education efforts. The trail is well-traveled but not crowded. This is actually an undiscovered jewel in the park.

TO GET THERE: From the intersection of Highway 73 (Little River Road) and Laurel Creek Road, go 0.2 mile toward Cades Cove (west) and turn at the Tremont sign. Follow the Tremont Road 2 miles to the Great Smoky Mountains Institute at Tremont (www.gsmit.org) which is on the left across the Middle Prong of the Little River. Turn left and cross the bridge to park at the Institute parking lot. The office has a park bookstore and a public restroom.

Walk up the first gravel driveway on the left toward the Lumber Ridge trailhead, just left of the Tremont dormitory. Follow Lumber Ridge Trail less than 100 feet to where the trail to the falls begins on the right. After 0.2 mile the falls trail turns left and climbs the side of the ridge past the water tank for the Institute. The trail is high above the Middle Prong of the Little River (sometimes more than 300 feet). A couple of wet weather branches that drain the steep slopes of Mill Ridge are crossed. The first part of the trail is steep but soon moderates. Return to the parking area by the same route.

WHITE OAK FLATS CASCADES

- **CASCADE**
- **50 FOOT FALL/120 FOOT RUN**
- **ROADSIDE**

*T*his wetter weather cascade provides a nice show right on the road. In dry weather it is a mostly damp, green trickle. However, in wet seasons and after summer rains it is a very nice cascade. The waters of White Oak Flats Branch slide down from White Oak Flats over multi-layered Metcalf Phyllite. The rock is largely moss-covered. The cascades are framed in straight tuliptrees with profusions of doghobble, rhodo-dendron, and wild hydrangea mixed in. The stream is 25

White Oak Flats Cascades

feet wide nearly the entire length of the cascade. The water flows under the road and into the Little River.

TO GET THERE: White Oak Flats Cascade is located on the south side of Little River Road (Highway 73) 0.5 mile from the Townsend "Y" going toward Gatlinburg. This is 16.5 miles from the intersection of the Newfound Gap Road (US 441) and the Little River Road at the Sugarlands Visitor Center. There are pull offs on the river side of the Little River Road on either side of the bridge under which White Oak Flats Branch flows. Use these pull offs to observe the cascade. Do not slow down or stop in the road!

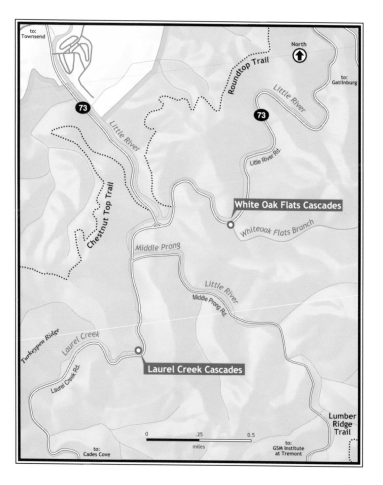

Waterfalls
OF THE SMOKIES
CHEROKEE–DEEP CREEK

CHEROKEE–DEEP CREEK

Oconaluftee means "by the river" in the Cherokee language. The Cherokee–Deep Creek area abounds in water, cascades and falls. Cherokee is on the park's southern boundary at the junction of Highways 441 and 19 about 30 miles from Gatlinburg. It's in the Qualla Boundary which is the home of the Eastern Band of Cherokees. In the town of Cherokee are numerous opportunities to learn of the Smokies' original native American inhabitants.

The Oconaluftee Visitor Center is at the park's southern entrance on Highway 441 (Newfound Gap Road) near Cherokee. The Mountain Farm Museum is a good interpretation of life in the 1800s, as is nearby Mingus Mill. The southern terminus of the Blue Ridge Parkway is at Cherokee. This 469-mile-long national parkway gives access to some of the most beautiful mountain scenery in the eastern United States.

National park campgrounds near Cherokee are Smokemont (on Newfound Gap Road 3.2 miles north of the visitor center), Balsam Mountain (9 miles off the Blue Ridge Parkway), and Deep Creek (near Bryson City). These three campgrounds usually don't have the crowds of those on the Tennessee side.

The Deep Creek Campground is located north of Bryson City on Deep Creek. Take Highway 19 south 10 miles from Cherokee to Bryson City. Turn right onto Everett Street in downtown Bryson City. At 0.2 mile turn right onto Depot Street then turn left onto Ramseur Street. After another immediate turn to the right, the road becomes curvy. Follow the signs to the Deep

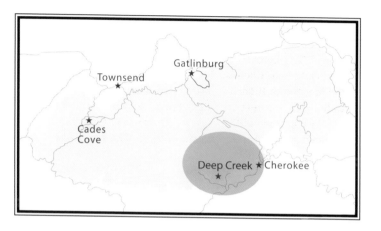

Creek Campground, which is 4 miles from Bryson City.

Four beautiful falls are in the immediate area of the Deep Creek Campground. The creek itself is well named with a large flow of water year round. Horace Kephart, noted writer and early advocate for a national park in the Smokies, last lived at Bryson Place on Deep Creek.

Smokemont Campground is near the junction of Bradley Fork and the Oconaluftee River. It's popular and often crowded, but is open all year, unlike Deep Creek and Balsam Mountain which are closed in the winter. Balsam Mountain is the highest campground in the park. It's perfect for a cool night's camping in the heat of the summer. To reach Balsam Mountain

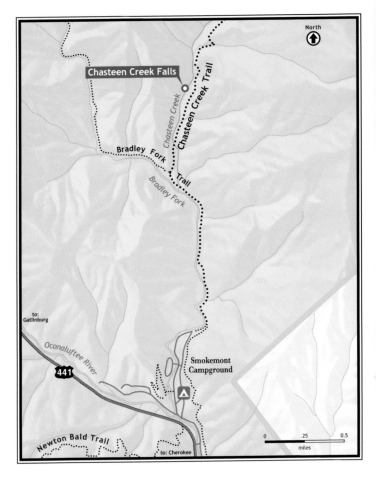

North

Chasteen Creek Falls

Chasteen Creek Trail

Chasteen Creek

Bradley Fork Trail

Bradley Fork

to: Gatlinburg

Oconaluftee River

441

Smokemont Campground

Newton Bald Trail

to: Cherokee

0   .25   0.5
miles

Campground drive 11 miles on the Blue Ridge Parkway from
Cherokee. Turn onto Heintooga Ridge Road.

CHASTEEN CREEK FALLS
- **CASCADE**
- **15 FOOT DROP, 50 FOOT RUN**
- **4 MILE ROUNDTRIP MODERATE HIKE**

*L*ying near the Greenbrier Fault, Chasteen Creek Falls
is a picturesque cascade in a lovely setting. The small
creek slides 50 feet down smoothly worn sandstone. The 20
foot wide stream spreads to nearly twice that width before
the banks of the creek at the cascade's base squeeze the
water back together. Notice the 2 inch thick streak of quartz
on the large rock at the top left of the cascade. Since the cascade is inclined at only 25°, the fall of the water is not very
great.

Large hemlocks in a primarily second growth hardwood

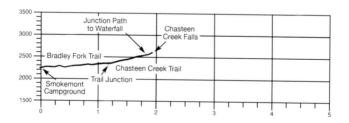

Chasteen Creek Falls

forest provide a shaded setting for doghobble and rhododendron to grow. Although this cascade doesn't have the dramatic plunge that others have, it's a wonderful spot for a picnic.

Chasteen Creek's headwaters are on the slopes of Hughes and Mine ridges. The valley formed by the creek is wide and open. Numerous house sites attest to the cultivation and subsequent logging of the area. Chasteen Creek is named for Chasteen Reagan who lived in the area with his family.

TO GET THERE: Begin at the northeast end of Smokemont Campground on the Bradley Fork Trail. Walk 1.2 miles up the wide road/trail to a junction with Chasteen Creek Trail. The first mile is beside Bradley Fork, which is named for early settlers of the area. Several benches are beside the stream.

Turn onto the Chasteen Creek Trail, which veers to the right. Soon after the trail intersection is backcountry campsite #50. Continue up Chasteen Creek Trail for 0.6 mile. A foot trail leaves the horse trail on the left at an old horse rack. Take the 0.2 mile foot trail around to the cascade. Return by the same route.

FLAT CREEK FALLS
- **CASCADE**
- **200+ FOOT DROP**
- **ROADSIDE**

The creek leaves the Flat Creek area to fall over 200 feet off Balsam Mountain in a 20 foot wide stream. The exposed rock over which the water rushes is part of the Thunderhead Formation which is prevalent in the park. This cascade is such a long one that one can not see the bottom from the top. Mountain laurel overhangs the creek above the falls. The falls can be seen across the deep, steep-sided valley from the Heintooga Ridge Road. The Flat Creek Trail runs near the top of the falls, but the best views are from the road.

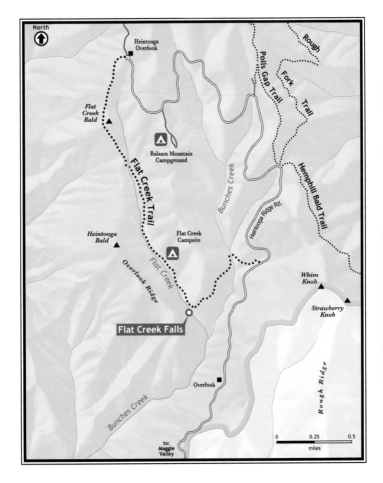

North

Heintooga
Overlook

Flat
Creek
Bald

Balsam Mountain
Campground

Flat Creek Trail

Bunches Creek

Polls Gap Trail

Rough

Fork

Trail

Hemphill Bald Trail

Heintooga Ridge Rd.

Heintooga
Bald

Flat Creek
Campsite

Flat Creek

Overlook Ridge

Flat Creek Falls

Whim
Knob

Strawberry
Knob

Bunches Creek

Overlook

Rough Ridge

to:
Maggie
Valley

0   0.25   0.5
miles

Flat Creek Falls

In fact, there is no maintained trail to the falls due to very dangerous, slippery conditions near the top of the falls.

TO GET THERE: Turn onto the Heintooga Ridge Road off the Blue Ridge Parkway 11 miles from Cherokee. A gravel overlook on the left about 3.5 miles from the Blue Ridge Parkway affords a nice view of the falls. In the summer the vegetation obscures the view. In the winter the Balsam Mountain Road is closed. Often the Blue Ridge Parkway is closed from Cherokee to Soco Gap. A winter hike or bicycle ride along the Balsam Mountain Road is a 7-8 mile roundtrip to get the best view of the falls— no leaves to obscure the falls and plenty of water flow.

INDIAN CREEK FALLS
- **CASCADE**
- **25 FOOT DROP, 45 FOOT RUN**
- **1.6 MILE ROUNDTRIP EASY HIKE**

A large plunge pool is at the base of the 45 foot Indian Creek Falls. The water slides down a 45° slope of Thunderhead Sandstone to form a beautiful cascade that is framed by rosebay rhododendron. The main flow is on the left with the stream on the right obscured by overhanging vegetation. The 25 foot wide stream broadens to 35 feet at the base.

The jumble of rocks on the right bank comes from the road above the falls. A "motor trail" was to have been constructed but was later abandoned by the Park

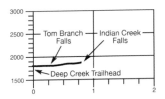

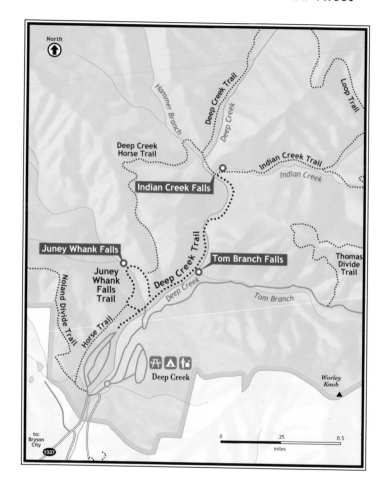

North

Deep Creek Trail

Hammer Branch

Deep Creek

Loop Trail

Deep Creek Horse Trail

Indian Creek Trail

Indian Creek Falls

Indian Creek

Juney Whank Falls

Deep Creek Trail

Tom Branch Falls

Juney Whank Falls Trail

Deep Creek

Thomas Divide Trail

Noland Divide Trail

Tom Branch

Horse Trail

Deep Creek

Worley Knob

to: Bryson City

1337

0   .25   0.5
miles

Indian Creek Falls

Service in order to better preserve the area. Wildflowers and rhododendron bloom in abundance along Indian and Deep creeks. Sit on the bench above the falls for a good view. A small side trail goes to the plunge pool at the base of Indian Creek Falls.

TO GET THERE: Begin at the parking area which is 0.6 mile upstream from the Deep Creek entrance to the park. Pass the entrance to the campground and the picnic area. The trail begins on the upper end of the parking area. A trail to Juney Whank Falls is to the left. It is possible to walk to Juney Whank and then loop down to the Deep Creek Trail. The direct route to Indian Creek Falls is to take the Deep Creek Trail. This is an old roadbed with a wide tread and gentle slope that is open to bicyclists as well as hikers. Tom Branch Falls is to the right after 0.25 mile. Continue on the Deep Creek Trail to Indian Creek Trail and Indian Creek Falls.

Deep Creek is crossed on a wide bridge at 0.4 mile. At the trail divide (0.8 mile) take the right fork onto Indian Creek Trail. The falls is only 100 yards from the junction. A small side trail on the left leads down to the falls. Return to the parking area along the same route.

JUNEY WHANK FALLS
- **CASCADE**
- **80 FOOT DROP, 125 FOOT RUN**
- **0.6 MILE EASY LOOP WALK**

A footbridge crosses Juney Whank Branch near the middle of this 125 foot cascade. Stand on the bridge to experience the water all around you. The creek flows through a 3 foot wide opening in the rocks at the top, then spreads to a width of 20 feet at the footlog. The main flow is on the right side with a lesser stream on the left. A thin film of water spreads between the two. The creek narrows to 6 feet as it travels down the ridge.

The first 20 feet is an easy slope before Juney Whank Branch falls 30 feet over Thunderhead Sandstone, which has horizontal streaks of quartz and vertical cracks. The incline is not as steep under the footlog, but it then drops another 45 feet through rocks and fallen timber. The rocks are moss covered and surrounded with doghobble.

The name Juney Whank is an unusual one. Some say it's Cherokee for "The bear went that-a-way." The Cherokee word for "bear" is "yonah" or "juna." However, the more likely explanation is that Junaluska Whank, who was named for the famed Cherokee chief, Junaluska, lived in this area. Junaluska Whank was called Juney by friends and neighbors. He is supposedly buried somewhere near the falls.

A small 20 foot cascade is downstream from the falls. From that vantage point is a good view of Juney Whank Falls. Juney Whank is a wonderful short walk that fits in well with an overnight stay at Deep Creek Campground or a hike to Indian Creek Falls.

TO GET THERE: The trail begins at the upper end of the parking area beyond the Deep Creek Camp-

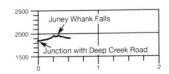

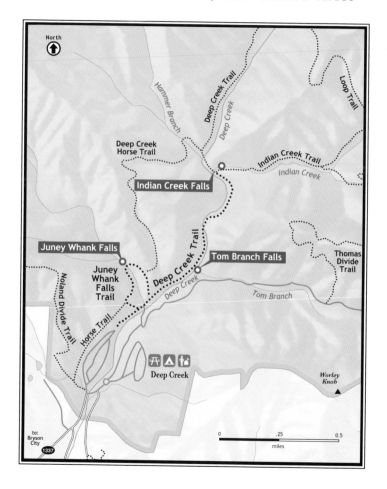

North

Hammer Branch

Deep Creek Trail

Deep Creek

Loop Trail

Deep Creek Horse Trail

Indian Creek Trail

Indian Creek Falls

Indian Creek

Deep Creek Trail

Juney Whank Falls

Tom Branch Falls

Thomas Divide Trail

Noland Divide Trail

Juney Whank Falls Trail

Deep Creek Trail

Deep Creek

Tom Branch

Horse Trail

Deep Creek

Worley Knob

to: Bryson City

1337

0   .25   0.5

miles

Juney Whank Falls

ground and Picnic Area, 0.6 mile from the park entrance. The easy walk through a mostly hardwood forest is a fun way to listen to the many birds that live in the Smokies. The trail climbs to a wider trail at 0.1 mile. Turn right onto it, then take another right on a side trail down to the footbridge and falls. Cross the bridge to intersect the horse trail, turn right and descend 50 feet. Take another right down to the Deep Creek Trail. Upon reaching Deep Creek turn left to walk to Tom Branch Falls and Indian Creek Falls or turn right to return to the parking area.

LITTLE CREEK FALLS

- **CASCADE**
- **95 FOOT DROP**
- **13.6 MILE ROUNDTRIP DIFFICULT HIKE**

This falls is well worth the difficult walk. Hundreds of small shelves are formed from stratified sandstone of the Thunderhead Formation. The layers of rock are horizontal. The water of Little Creek presents a big show as it falls off the side of Thomas Ridge near Deeplow Gap.

The main flow of water falls straight down the middle of the rock with a lesser stream to the left. The 25 foot wide cascade spreads to 40 feet at its base, where a log acts as both dam and bridge making a small pool and a way across the creek. Moss covered logs and rhododendron frame this pic-

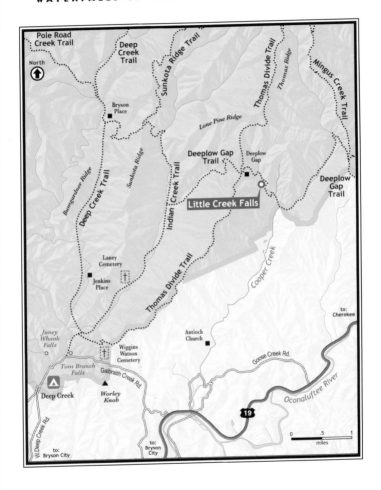

ture of falling water. Doghobble and ferns are in abundance in the primarily hardwood forest.

The trail passes near the top of the falls and crosses the creek at the base. It's amazing that such a small creek can create such a large wonder.

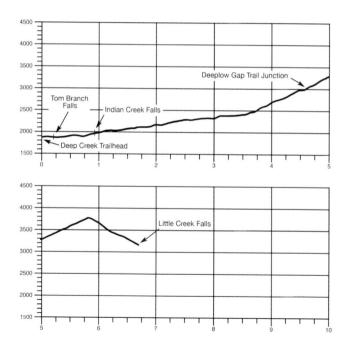

Little Creek Falls

TO GET THERE: The route is steep, difficult walking and begins at the Deep Creek Campground. Walk up the Deep Creek Trail past Tom Branch Falls 0.75 mile to Indian Creek Trail. Turn right onto Indian Creek Trail near Indian Creek Falls. Both trails are jeep roads that provide easy walking. The Indian Creek Trail follows its namesake, ascending 3.7 miles to Deeplow Gap Trail.

Follow Deeplow Gap Trail 2.4 miles to the falls. You will first climb Thomas Ridge on a graded roadbed. After 0.3 mile, the trail goes to the left but the road veers right. Leave the road to go up Deeplow Gap Trail and reach Deeplow Gap at mile 5.8. The trail intersects the Thomas Divide Trail here. Continue east (straight ahead) on Deeplow Gap Trail to descend along Little Creek. The top of the cascade is reached at 6.5 miles and the bottom is 0.2 mile on down after a switchback.

MINGO FALLS

- **CASCADE**
- **180 FOOT DROP**
- **0.4 MILE ROUNDTRIP MODERATE WALK**

*T*his magnificent fall of water actually lies outside the boundaries of the park, within the Qualla Boundary. Since it's included in the park's literature and is the most spectacular sight in the area, it had to be a part of this book.

The water of Mingo Creek drops 180 feet over a bare sandstone ledge which is on the Greenbrier Fault. The rock is highly stratified, slanting down from the left to the right at about 15°. This sandstone is inclined away from the viewer at 45° back into the mountain. The water splashes over hundreds of small shelves.

At the top, the falls begin as an 8 foot wide stream. Tiny streamlets stray off to the right side of the bare rock face while the main force of the water stays to the left. The whole cascade widens to 40 feet at the base.

A bare rock cliff to the left of the falls is separated from the creek by pine and mountain laurel. Notice that at the base of the falls the vegetation is mainly rhododendron and hemlock, but at the top it's pine and mountain laurel.

A small bridge and bench provide excellent spots for photographing or simply enjoying the magnificent sight. A trail does go to the top, but the view is not as good as from the base.

TO GET THERE: Take the Big Cove Road which begins 2.5 miles south of the Oconaluftee Visitor Center on Highway 441. Go on the Big Cove Road under the Blue Ridge Parkway 5 miles to the Mingo Falls Campground which is on the right. Cross the bridge to the campground. Parking is available to hikers.

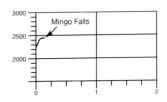

The trail begins to the left of the water plant for

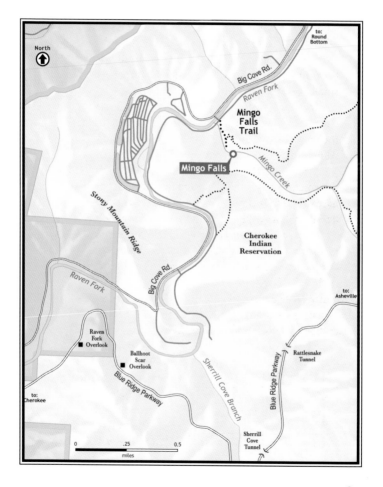

North

to:
Round
Bottom

Big Cove Rd.

Raven Fork

Mingo
Falls
Trail

Mingo Falls

Mingo Creek

Stony Mountain Ridge

Cherokee
Indian
Reservation

Raven Fork

Big Cove Rd.

to:
Asheville

Raven
Fork
Overlook

Ballhoot
Scar
Overlook

Sherrill Cove Branch

Blue Ridge Parkway

Rattlesnake
Tunnel

Blue Ridge Parkway

to:
Cherokee

Blue Ridge Parkway

Sherrill
Cove
Tunnel

0   .25   0.5
miles

Mingo Falls

the campground. The first 200 yards are very steep. Several benches are provided to make the ascent easier. The trail levels off to follow the creek around to the base of the falls.

The trail to the top begins at the top of the steep part which is halfway to the base of the falls. It goes up the ridge about 0.25 mile to the head of the falls. After a switchback a small trail veers to the right. Follow this smaller trail away from what appears to be the main trail. This little trail goes to the top where a fence provides moderate protection on the steep, bare rock. DO NOT FOLLOW OTHER TRAILS DOWN. GO BACK THE WAY YOU CAME.

This sight is easily reached and should not be missed.

SWEAT HEIFER CASCADES
- **CASCADE**
- **40 FOOT DROP, 125 FOOT RUN**
- **7.3 OR 7.6 MILE DIFFICULT HIKE**

This cascade tumbles over rock of the Anakeesta Formation to make a beautiful show on the slopes of the high Smokies. Sweat Heifer Trail crosses at the top of the cascade. However, the best views are from the trail as you approach the falls from below. Several small waterfalls are upstream from the trail.

Just below the trail crossing, the creek spreads out to cascade over stratified, gray rock of the Anakeesta Formation.

The main flow stays to the right but some water spreads to cover a 50-foot-wide area of mossy stone. Halfway down, the water hits a small shelf and slides to the left forming a nice pool at the bottom. One hundred feet downstream from the pool is another cascade that drops 6 feet and is 3 to 5 feet wide. Sweat Heifer Creek continues to cascade down the mountain. The cascade is framed by yellow birch, beech, and rhododendron. In the summer look for bee balm, dodder, and wild hydrangea. Any time of year, this cascade is a delight.

TO GET THERE:

There are two ways to reach Sweat Heifer Cascades and both routes are steep and difficult. The easier of the two begins at the Kephart Prong Trailhead on Newfound Gap Road, 5 miles north from Smokemont Campground and 8.5 miles south of Newfound Gap. A small parking area is on the east side of the road at a prominent footbridge over the Oconaluftee River. Take the Kephart Prong Trail 2 miles to the Kephart Prong Shelter. This walk climbs 850 feet on an old road that passes the remnants of a Civilian Conservaton Corps (CCC) camp (1933-1942). Notice the boxwoods, chimney, walls, and day lilies which all are evidence of the large camp. Farther up the trail are the remains of a fish hatchery run by the Works Progress Administration (WPA) in the 1930s. Farther on are rails which were a part of the logging railroad operated by the Champion Fibre Company in the 1920s.

A thin cascade drops from the side of the ridge beyond the

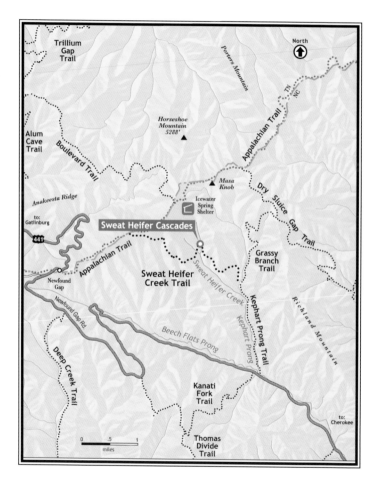

Trillium
Gap
Trail

Porters Mountain

North

Alum
Cave
Trail

Boulevard Trail

Horseshoe
Mountain
5288'

Appalachian Trail

TN
NC

Anakeesta Ridge

Masa
Knob

Dry Sluice Gap Trail

Icewater
Spring
Shelter

to:
Gatlinburg

441

Sweat Heifer Cascades

Appalachian Trail

Sweat Heifer
Creek Trail

Sweat Heifer Creek

Grassy
Branch
Trail

Newfound Gap

Kephart Prong Trail

Richland Mountain

Newfound Gap Rd.

Beech Flats Prong

Kephart Prong

Deep Creek Trail

Kanati
Fork
Trail

to:
Cherokee

0   .5   1
miles

Thomas
Divide
Trail

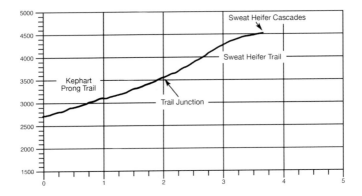

third footlog. Kephart Prong is a wonderful display of water, stones, and cascades. The trail is wide and follows the stream.

At 2 miles is the Kephart Prong Shelter named for Horace Kephart, an author and early advocate for the formation of Great Smoky Mountains National Park. Take the Sweat Heifer Creek Trail to the left. The next 1.6 miles are steeper, gaining a little over 1,000 feet. The trail winds uphill sometimes on an old roadbed. Sweat Heifer Cascades is reached at 3.6 miles from the trailhead. Return by the same route.

The more difficult route begins on the Appalachian Trail (AT) at Newfound Gap. Walk northeast on the AT toward Charlies Bunion. The trail steadily climbs about 900 feet in 1.7 miles with occasional views of the North Carolina side of the park. Turn right at the junction with Sweat Heifer Creek Trail.

Sweat Heifer Cascades

The trail descends 1,300 feet to cross Sweat Heifer Creek at the cascade. About 0.4 mile before the cascade, the trail crosses a small tributary. On the left is a nice twin cascade that falls 20 feet to the level of the trail. The return trip to Newfound Gap is uphill for 2 miles to the AT then downhill to the parking area.

Another possibility is to use two cars, parking one at Newfound Gap and the other at Kephart Prong Trailhead. This route is 7.4 miles and an excellent alternative.

THREE WATERFALLS LOOP

- **CASCADES**
- **25 FOOT & 80 FOOT DROPS**
- **2.4 MILE MODERATE LOOP HIKE**

*T*his pleasant little loop trail offers a variety of sights, from waterfalls to wildflowers to relative solitude in a forested setting. Not many trails in Great Smoky Mountains National Park offer so many highlights with so little effort. The waterfalls will be most scenic after it has rained.

TO GET THERE: Begin at the parking area which is 0.6 mile upstream from the Deep Creek entrance to the park. Pass the entrance to the campground and the picnic area. Start the loop by walking the short Juney Whank Falls Trail to Juney Whank Falls (see the Juney Whank narrative for origins of the name). Signs at each trail junction direct you to the "falls." After 0.3

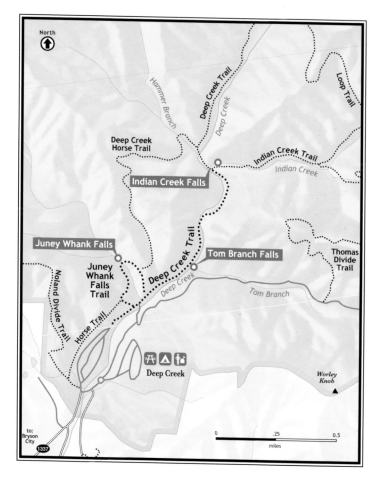

North

Hommer Branch

Deep Creek Trail

Deep Creek

Loop Trail

Deep Creek Horse Trail

Indian Creek Trail

Indian Creek

Indian Creek Falls

Juney Whank Falls

Deep Creek Trail

Tom Branch Falls

Thomas Divide Trail

Juney Whank Falls Trail

Noland Divide Trail

Horse Trail

Deep Creek

Tom Branch

Deep Creek

Worley Knob

to: Bryson City

1337

0   .25   0.5

miles

93

mile, 7 steps and a narrow path leave the graded roadbed and lead down to the waterfall and a footbridge across Juney Whank Branch.

The footbridge makes an excellent place to view the scenic falls. Water cascades across bedrock for 40 feet above the bridge and 50 feet below. Continue across the bridge and up the bank. After 100 yards you reach a trail junction; take the left fork and follow Deep Creek Horse Trail.

You climb steadily 0.5 mile to a pleasant gap, then descend steeply until you pick up pretty Hammer Branch. Turn right at the trail junction (left goes to a cemetery). Hammer Branch was probably named for a hammer or pounding mill that once existed along it. Hammer mills were ingenious mechanisms used by many farm families in the mountains. They were basically large mortar and pestles powered by running water that slowly crushed corn into meal.

At the junction with Deep Creek Trail, turn right and follow Deep Creek Trail 0.1 mile to Indian Creek Trail. Take Indian Creek Trail "200 feet" to beautiful Indian Creek Falls. It's an elegant cascade with a large deep pool at its base. After you

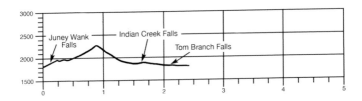

enjoy the falls, backtrack to Deep Creek Trail. Turn left, and follow Deep Creek Trail as it runs beside scenic Deep Creek 0.7 mile to the trailhead. At about 0.2 mile before trail's end, make sure to take in Tom Branch Falls, which tumbles into Deep Creek at the far side of the creek. Vegetation obscures much of the waterfall during summer, so watch closely.

TOM BRANCH FALLS
- **CASCADE**
- **80 FOOT DROP**
- **0.5 MILE ROUNDTRIP EASY WALK**

*S*it on the bench beside Deep Creek opposite Tom Branch Falls to best observe this marvelous cascade. Two small steps at the top begin the more than 80 foot fall into Deep Creek. The water flows over stratified sandstone onto two larger and more widely spaced steps before hitting a last shelf above the rushing creek.

The stream starts on the right, shifts to the left for most of the trip down, and then returns to the right before the final shelf divides it into two streams. Tom Branch Falls is 3 feet wide at the head of the cascade,

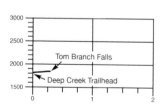

Tom Branch Falls

widens to 8 feet in the midsection and spreads to 10 feet at the base.

The origin of the name has been difficult to track down, but it has been suggested that it was named for Tom Wiggins, a Civil War veteran who lived on the stream from 1854 to 1892. Wiggins had a house and a grist mill on the small branch.

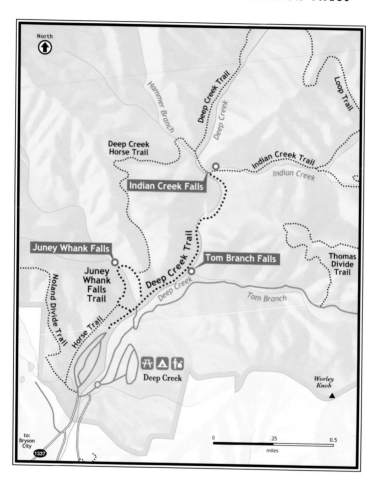

North

Hammer Branch

Deep Creek Trail

Deep Creek

Loop Trail

Deep Creek Horse Trail

Indian Creek Falls

Indian Creek Trail

Indian Creek

Juney Whank Falls

Deep Creek Trail

Tom Branch Falls

Thomas Divide Trail

Juney Whank Falls Trail

Deep Creek

Tom Branch

Noland Divide Trail

Horse Trail

Deep Creek

Worley Knob

to: Bryson City

1337

0   .25   0.5
miles

TO GET THERE: Begin at the parking area which is 0.6 mile upstream from the Deep Creek entrance to the park. Pass the entrance to the campground and the picnic area. The trail begins on the upper end of the parking area. A trail to Juney Whank Falls is to the left. It is possible to walk to Juney Whank and then loop down to the Deep Creek Trail. The direct route to Tom Branch Falls is to take the Deep Creek Trail. This is an old roadbed with a wide tread and gentle slope that is open to bicyclists as well as hikers. Tom Branch drops off the ridge on the right side of Deep Creek opposite the trail 0.25 mile from the trailhead at the parking area. Continue on the Deep Creek Trail for 0.8 mile to Indian Creek Trail and Indian Creek Falls for a look at another waterfall.

Waterfalls

OF THE SMOKIES

CLINGMANS DOME

CLINGMANS DOME

Clingmans Dome is the highest peak in Great Smoky Mountains National Park at 6,643 feet. In spite of its great height, it's the most accessible summit due to a paved road which leads nearly to the top. An observation tower affords fantastic views which are available to everyone who is willing to stroll the 0.5 mile through the spruce-fir forest of the high Smokies. The Appalachian Trail is at the highest point of its entire 2,100 mile length at Clingmans Dome. Not many falls are close to the crest of the Great Smokies. However, Forney Creek Cascade is beautiful.

Turn onto the 7 mile Clingmans Dome Road as it leaves Highway 441 at Newfound Gap. This intersection is 27 miles from Cherokee and 22 miles from Gatlinburg. The Clingmans Dome Road is closed in the winter (from Nov. to April). Plenty of parking is available at the Forney Ridge parking area.

FORNEY CREEK CASCADE
- **CASCADE**
- **85 FOOT DROP, 245 FOOT RUN**
- **6 MILE STRENUOUS HIKE**

Forney Creek Cascade is a combination of two slides of water over quartz-streaked sandstone. The water flows through a 2 foot opening in a jumble of rocks, then begins a 110 foot cascade down the first incline. The coarse-

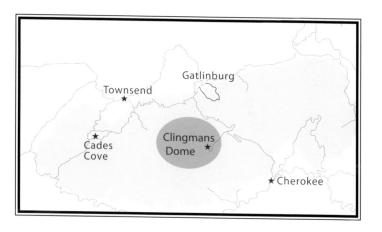

grained sandstone has been smoothed by the creek. The rock is crisscrossed with quartz streaks 3 to 4 inches thick. The creek quickly spreads to 15 feet then on to 25 feet. The main flow of water stays to the left as it slips into a shallow pool.

The creek narrows to 5 feet before it begins its descent again. This time it cascades 135 feet spreading to 55 feet as it enters a shallow pool. The upper section is steeper than the lower one. A small creek pours into the plunge pool on the right at the base of the cascade. A large railroad rail from the turn of the 20th century logging boom is twisted in the rocks at the base.

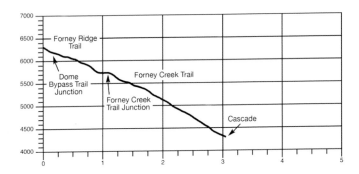

TO GET THERE: The hike begins at the Forney Ridge parking area at the end of Clingmans Dome Road. Use the Forney Ridge Trail which begins to the left of the paved trail to Clingmans Dome (near the bulletin board). The Forney Ridge Trail is a rocky walk, so wear good shoes or boots. Descend 0.1 mile to a trail divide. Take the left trail to descend the western slope of Forney Ridge. This is through the spruce-fir forest which is fighting for survival against the balsam wooly adelgid.

Take the Forney Creek Trail which turns off to the right at 1.1 miles. The Forney Ridge Trail continues straight ahead to Andrews Bald which is about 1 mile from the trail junction. To reach the falls, descend the Forney Creek Trail. The forest opens after a set of switchbacks to reveal sparse undergrowth beneath second growth hardwoods. A forest fire in the 1920s swept this area. A steep graded incline crosses the trail. This

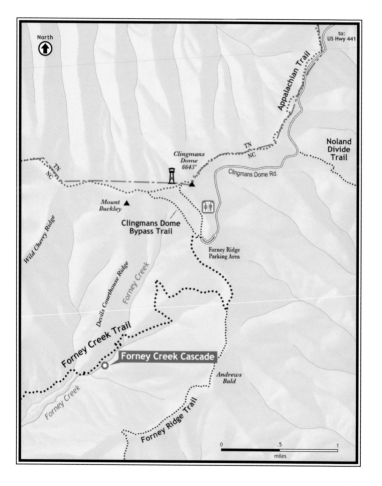

North

to:
US Hwy 441

Appalachian Trail

Noland
Divide
Trail

Clingmans
Dome
6643'

TN
NC

Clingmans Dome Rd.

Mount
Buckley

Clingmans Dome
Bypass Trail

TN
NC

Wild Cherry Ridge

Devils Courthouse Ridge

Forney Creek

Forney Ridge
Parking Area

Forney Creek Trail

Forney Creek Cascade

Forney Creek

Andrews
Bald

Forney Ridge Trail

0   .5   1
miles

Forney Creek Cascade

was used by the Norwood Lumber Company in its logging operations.

The trail meets a small stream 1.4 miles from the trail intersection. Here the trail follows the creek down the valley toward Forney Creek. After 0.7 mile the trail crosses the upper part of Forney Creek. Rails and other artifacts are scattered about this crossing. The trail stays above the creek for 200 yards before descending to the cascade beside Backcountry Campsite #68. Have a good rest. As you have no doubt ascertained, the walk back is all uphill.

ROAD PRONG CASCADE
- **CASCADE**
- **70 FOOT RUN, 50 FOOT DROP**
- **2.6 MILE MODERATE HIKE**

*T*his is a spectacular display of stone and water in an easy to reach place. Road Prong churns white as it falls over rocks of the Thunderhead Formation. This cascade is near the Mingus Fault that runs off the Oconaluftee Fault. The stream is about 18 feet wide at the top but spreads to nearly 25 feet at the base. A small plunge pool slows the water momentarily before it rushes downstream to several other smaller cascades that are a little difficult to see from the trail. This cascade has also been called Trickling Falls. However, there does not appear to be an official name on

USGS maps. A very nice cascade with a 6 foot drop and a 25 foot run is only 75 feet upstream from the large cascade.

TO GET THERE: Begin at the Chimney Tops Parking Area which is 6.7 miles south from the Sugarlands Visitor Center on Newfound Gap Road. Cross Walker Camp Prong just below the parking area. You will cross Road Prong three times on bridges as you climb to the trail junction. At 0.9 mile go left onto Road Prong Trail. This trail and creek get their name from the old road that went over the Smokies at this place. This was the main route over the mountains from Sevierville to Cherokee in the late 1800s and early 1900s. The trail generally stays near Road Prong to the large cascade. There are two good spots to see the cascade downstream. The trail climbs up beside the cascade. It is important to stay on the trail because the rocks can be very slippery. This is best viewed in the winter when

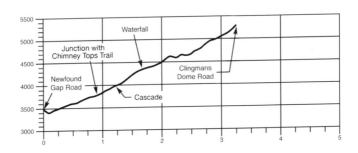

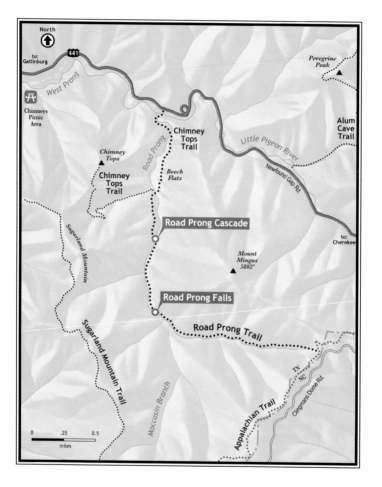

North

to:
Gatlinburg

441

West Prong

Chimneys
Picnic
Area

Chimney
Tops

Chimney
Tops
Trail

Road Prong

Chimney
Tops
Trail

Beech
Flats

Little Pigeon River

Peregrine
Peak

Alum
Cave
Trail

Newfound Gap Rd.

to:
Cherokee

Road Prong Cascade

Mount
Mingus
5802'

Road Prong Falls

Sugarland Mountain

Sugarland Mountain Trail

Road Prong Trail

Moccasin Branch

Appalachian Trail

TN
NC

Clingmans Dome Rd.

0   .25   0.5
miles

Road Prong Cascade

leaves are off the trees and the water flow is good. Also, there are wonderful ice and snow scenes at this cascade in the coldest weather. This is a great spring hike due to the many wildflowers. Several beautiful cascades are above this large cascade. Before turning around be sure to walk on up to Road Prong Falls. Return to your car along the same route.

ROAD PRONG FALLS

- **FALLS**
- **15 FOOT DROP**
- **3.3 MILE MODERATE HIKE**

*T*his is known in some of the older literature as Talking Falls, although there appears to be no official USGS name. It is a nice falls amid large boulders of meta-sandstone of the Thunderhead Formation that makes up the majority of the rock in the park. Road Prong squeezes through several large boulders to fall about 15 feet. The stream is only about 3 feet wide at this point but fans out to about 6 to 8 feet. The water flows into a large plunge pool. The falls is near the Oconaluftee Fault, one of the park's major faults. Pair this falls with its larger sibling downstream for a wonderful day of water and stone. Notice the difference in the rock at this falls and that at Road Prong Cascade. The

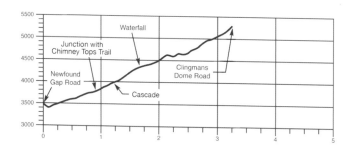

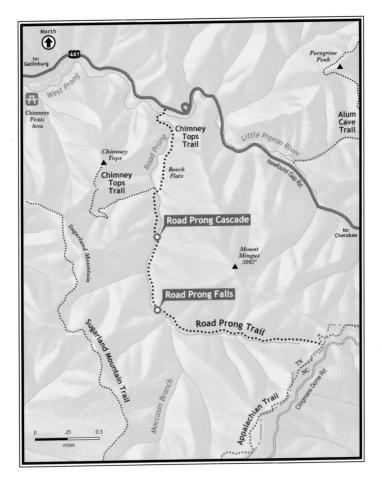

Road Prong Falls

second falls is well worth the extra distance. There are several nice cascades between the two.

Ken Wise in *Hiking Trails of the Great Smoky Mountains* tells the story of a young South Carolinian named Psatter who attempted to cross the Smokies in the 1850s. Caught in a winter storm, he took refuge under an overhanging rock at this falls. He froze to death under the rock and was later found by passing hunters who buried him near the trail.

TO GET THERE: Begin from the Road Prong Trailhead on Clingmans Dome Road, 2 miles west of Newfound Gap. Hike down Road Prong Trail 1.7 miles to the falls. If you can swing two cars, park one at Chimney Tops Trailhead on Newfound Gap Road and the other at Road Prong Trailhead. You will be able to take in Road Prong Falls and Cascade in the 3.3 mile downhill hike.

Waterfalls

OF THE SMOKIES

COSBY

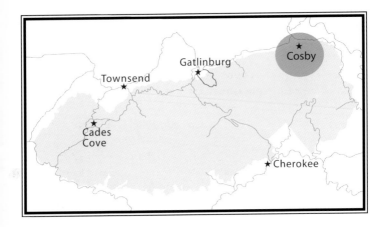

COSBY

Cosby is 19 miles east of Gatlinburg on Highway 321 and 8 miles from I-40 on the Foothills Parkway. The Cosby Campground road begins 1.5 miles from the intersection of Highway 321 with Highway 32. It's 2 miles from Highway 32 to the Cosby Campground and Picnic Area. The campground and picnic areas are rarely crowded, even in peak season.

HEN WALLOW FALLS

- **CASCADE**
- **95 FOOT DROP**
- **100 FOOT DROP, 285 FOOT RUN**
- **4.3 MILE ROUNDTRIP MODERATE HIKE**

*H*en Wallow Falls is a cascade 95 feet high. The water of Hen Wallow Creek slides down gray quartz-streaked sandstone of the Roaring Fork Formation. In drier weather, the cascade begins as two streams of water 6 feet apart and quickly merges to form a 30 foot stream at the base. Wetter weather enlarges the size and force considerably.

It's said that one origin of the name "Hen Wallow" is that ruffed grouse wallowed in the dust near here. The grouse, called "wood hen" by some, is known to engage in such behavior. Carson Brewer offers a more interesting explanation. He writes that Hen Wallow was the name one community gave to another after the first community had been dubbed Rooster-town. The names were based on a feud between communities.

Although this cascade doesn't carry a high volume of water, it's a pretty sight any time of year. It's one of the tallest in the park at nearly 100 feet.

TO GET THERE:

The trailhead is 2 miles from Highway 32 near the entrance to Cosby Campground. There is ample parking at the picnic area and Gabes Mountain Trail begins across the road. The first

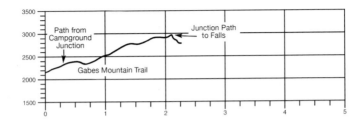

part of the hike is on a rocky roadbed which goes 0.3 mile until a feeder trail from the Cosby Campground enters from the left. Stay to the right to cross Rock Creek on a footlog. A log bench provides an opportunity to enjoy the song of the creek.

At 1.1 miles a small footbridge crosses Crying Creek onto an old roadbed. After 30 yards continue on the Gabes Mountain Trail to the left. Crying Creek is named because a man mistakenly shot his brother in the darkness and confusion of a bear hunt. The trail meanders around the northeastern slopes of Gabes Mountain. After 1.9 miles a modest branch flows under the trail forming a small waterfall of 6 to 8 feet. It's particularly pretty in the winter with no undergrowth and plenty of rain.

One quarter mile from the branch and 2.1 miles from the trailhead is the 800 foot side trail to the base of Hen Wallow Falls. Observe the warning signs! DO NOT CLIMB ON THE

Hen Wallow Falls

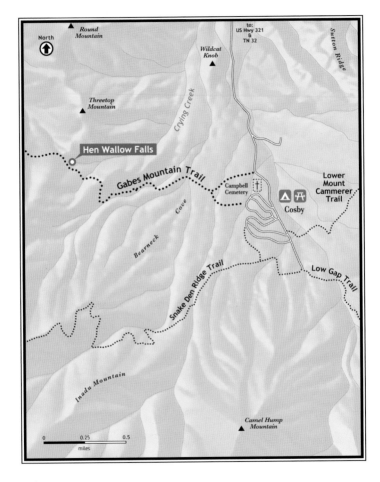

North

Round Mountain

Wildcat Knob

to:
US Hwy 321
&
TN 32

Sutton Ridge

Threetop Mountain

Crying Creek

Hen Wallow Falls

Gabes Mountain Trail

Campbell Cemetery

Cosby

Lower Mount Cammerer Trail

Bearneck Cove

Snake Den Ridge Trail

Low Gap Trail

Inadu Mountain

Camel Hump Mountain

0   0.25   0.5
miles

ROCKS! The view to the north (away from the falls) is of Round and Green mountains. Cosby can be seen in the distance.

This is a very enjoyable hike anytime of the year. It's a cool spot in the summer or colorful one in the fall.

NOISY CREEK CASCADES
•**CASCADE**
•**35 FOOT DROP, 70 FOOT RUN**
•**ROADSIDE**

*T*his wonderful cascade has a good flow of water year round. Its roadside location along Highway 321 on the national park's boundary makes it one of the easiest cascades to see. Noisy Creek falls to a bridge on the highway amid large moss covered rocks and boulders. These rocks are of Pigeon Siltstone, a fine-grained metasandstone. The cascade is on the Gatlinburg Fault, one of the major faults that formed the Smokies.

This cascade is surrounded by hemlocks, tuliptrees, and maples, with rhododendron greening the area year round. This is a beautiful cascade especially in high water flow periods. Its 30 foot width makes a scenic display as Noisy Creek splashes over large rocks.

TO GET THERE: Noisy Creek is on the park side (south) of Highway 321. It is 12 miles from Light #3 in Gatlinburg and 6.5

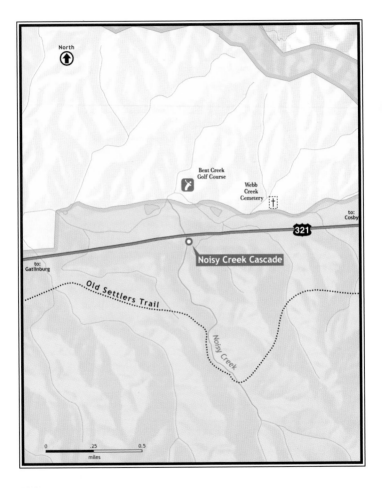

Noisy Creek Cascades

miles from the Cosby intersection of Highway 321 and Highway 32. Its location is actually at an odd place. Highway 321 goes uphill from either direction to cross Noisy Creek on a small rise. The creek appears to be running along the top of a small ridge rather than in a valley or hollow.

Waterfalls

OF THE SMOKIES

FONTANA

FONTANA

Fontana Village is a resort area that was built from the housing used by workers during the construction of Fontana Dam. On the west end of the park, follow Highway 129 from the Foothills Parkway or Maryville to Highway 28 at Deals Gap. Then turn onto Highway 28 for the 11 miles to Fontana. Beautiful overlooks abound on Highways 129 and 28 which go 24 miles from the intersection of 129 and the Foothills Parkway to Fontana Village. From Cherokee, take Highway 19 through Bryson City until it intersects Highway 28 which goes to Fontana.

Visit Fontana Dam, the highest dam in the Tennessee Valley Authority system at 480 feet. The dam was built in the 1940s to supply Alcoa and Oak Ridge with power. The Appalachian Trail passes over the dam on its way into the national park. Fontana is one of the quieter spots in the Smokies, attracting many fishermen to the lake and creeks.

HAZEL CREEK CASCADES
- **CASCADE**
- **25 FOOT AND 55 FOOT RUNS**
- **A 27 MILE OR 15 MILE ROUNDTRIP DIFFICULT HIKE**

The Hazel Creek Cascades are located on the far upper reaches of Hazel Creek on the western side of Welch Ridge. The water of Hazel Creek tumbles over Thunderhead

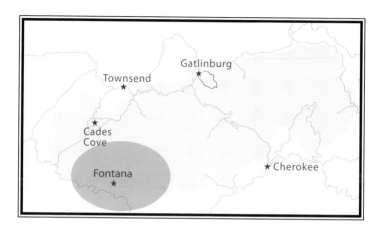

Sandstone ledges in a remote area. The Hazel Creek Trail crosses the creek just above the uppermost cascade. Here the creek moves to the left and then back to the right before falling over a 15 foot ledge. There is a small plunge pool as the creek continues downward. The creek narrows as it exits the pool and rushes down over rocks to another smaller ledge of 6 feet. After this drop into another small pool the creek squeezes into a 3-4 foot wide gutter frothing down another 8 feet in a 25 foot run. Rhododendron arch over this narrow channel.

The creek flows down 500 feet to another beautiful cascade where the water drops 20 vertical feet down the 55 foot slide. At this point the creek widens as it slips over Thunderhead

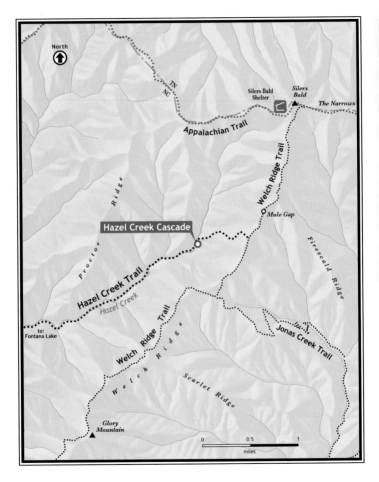

Hazel Creek Cascades

Sandstone which is a metamorphic rock that is more resistant to erosion. There is a large plunge pool at the base of this nice cascade. In the summer this lowest cascade is difficult to see from the trail due to undergrowth.

Although these cascades are small, they are quite beautiful in this most secluded of places. Few have discovered these precious gems.

TO GET THERE: For the 27 mile route begin at the Fontana Boat Dock outside Fontana Village. A boat can be hired any day from 8 a.m. to 3:30 p.m. year round. To make reservations call 1-800-849-2258. Cross the lake to the Hazel Creek Trail, which is a good roadbed. The walk along Hazel Creek is gentle and beautiful. Walk through historic Proctor, the site of logging operations in the early years of the 20th Century. Although very little remains of this once thriving community, over 1,000 people lived there in its boom days.

The trail follows Hazel Creek all the way up to the cascades. The grade is gentle but long. Numerous opportunities to enjoy the creek are available all along this very popular fishing stream. Anglers frequent the rushing waters for good catches. The remoteness of the area lends itself to an abundance of wildlife. Otters have made a comeback along the stream while brook trout swim its waters.

Evidence of the old logging days can be seen along the trail all the way to the cascades. Twisted and bent rails, steel cable, and an old railroad bed are at the foot of the cascades where a switchback of the old railroad bed goes up the side of the ridge. Five backcountry campsites are on the trail. Four of the sites are open to horses, one to foot travelers only. Spend a few days in this once populated, now remote region. Horace Kephart called the upper reaches of Hazel Creek, "The Back of Beyond."

Another route to the cascades drops down from above, beginning at the Forney Ridge parking area at Clingmans Dome. This second route is a strenuous hike on the Appalachian, Welch Ridge, and Hazel Creek trails. It affords many vistas into North Carolina and Tennessee. Walk up the paved trail to Clingmans Dome tower, then take the Appalachian Trail and follow it 4.1 miles to the Welch Ridge Trail that goes off to the left just east of Silers Bald.

Take the Welch Ridge Trail for 1.8 miles to its junction with

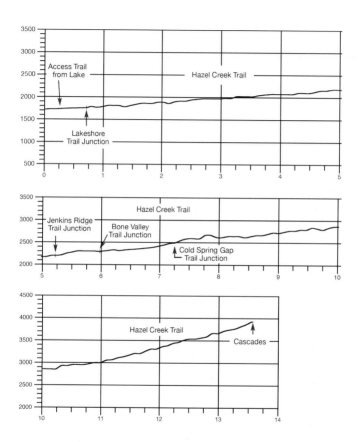

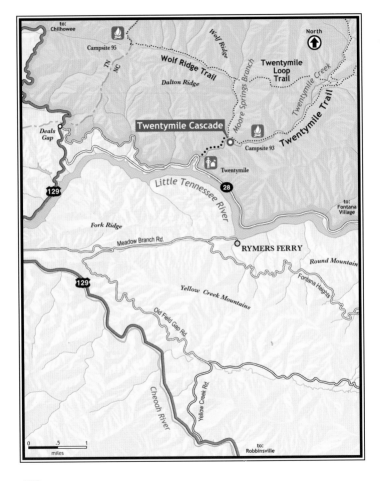

the Hazel Creek Trail to the right. It's 1.6 miles from this junction to the uppermost cascade. This part of the walk descends 1,000 feet in about a mile and a half. Remember the return trip to the parking lot gains over 3,000 feet over 7 miles of trail.

TWENTYMILE CASCADE

- **CASCADE**
- **22 FOOT DROP, 95 FOOT RUN**
- **1.25 MILE ROUNDTRIP EASY WALK**

Twentymile is an undisturbed, secluded spot in the park. Even though Twentymile Cascade is relatively small, it is beautiful. The cascade, which is 100 yards above the junction of Twentymile Creek and Moore Springs Branch, is a series of uneven ledges. The 20 foot wide creek spills over a series of zigzag ledges which act as switchbacks.

Notice the small, forceful flow to the left, undercutting the rocks and trees. When the water level is high, it surrounds a large boulder before forming a 25 foot diameter pool. The creek then drops 6 feet while running through a 20 foot boulder field.

After a drop of 4 feet over a moss covered ledge, the creek slides down a perfectly formed ledge. This last ledge is 12 feet high and 25 feet wide with a 45° tilt away from the base. This tilt allows the water to spread evenly and slide to the last pool. Twentymile Creek turns slightly to the right as large

Twentymile Cascade

boulders on the left squeeze it back to a normal size. This speeds the flow as the water rushes to meet Moore Springs Branch.

The exposed sandstone is crisscrossed with streaks of quartz. Above the main cascade (130 feet) is a small falls where the creek is only 10 feet wide. The water drops 6 feet over a rounded stone outcropping completely surrounding it with an even flow. In dry weather a stone splits the creek to form two small falls. The area is dense with rhododendron

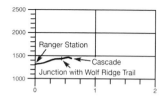

and hemlock which provide greenery all year round.

It's said Twentymile Creek gets its name because it is 20 miles downstream from the mouth of Hazel Creek. Others have said that it was because the creek was thought to drain 20 miles through the mountains.

This easy walk is a nice stop on the way to Fontana or after taking the Parson Branch Road out of Cades Cove.

TO GET THERE: The Twentymile Ranger Station is on North Carolina Highway 28, 3 miles east of the junction of Highway 129 at Deals Gap and 6.2 miles west of Fontana Dam. This is about 18.5 miles from the west end of the Foothills Parkway at Highway 129.

Two parking areas are available, one below the ranger station and one above. Follow the jeep road past the ranger station to the gate. This is an easy walk of 0.5 mile to the junction of Wolf Ridge Trail. Continue to the right for another 100 yards to the sign marking the Twentymile Cascade, which is below the trail to the right.

The entire trail is a wide gravel surface, which makes for easy walking. In spring, wildflowers abound including foamflower, trillium, fire pink, doghobble and buttercups. Return to the car by the same trail.

Waterfalls

OF THE SMOKIES

GATLINBURG–MT. LE CONTE

GATLINBURG–MT. LE CONTE

Gatlinburg, the northern gateway to the Smokies, is a popular tourist spot with many shops and attractions. The Gatlinburg Craftsman Loop is east of the town off Highway 321 on the way to Cosby. The Sugarlands Visitor Center is 2 miles from Gatlinburg on Highway 441 (Newfound Gap Road). A museum and movie are part of the services available at the visitor center which is next to the park headquarters.

From Interstate 40 take Highway 66 to Sevierville, Pigeon Forge, and Gatlinburg. Highway 321 also brings you to Gatlinburg from I-40 via Cosby. The bypass from Pigeon Forge to Sugarlands around Gatlinburg has scenic overlooks of Gatlinburg and Mt. Le Conte. This route is a real time saver during peak tourist season.

Mt. Le Conte, a popular hiking destination, is the third highest peak (6,593 feet) in the park. Two trails up Le Conte, Trillium Gap and Rainbow Falls, have spectacular waterfalls.

The Roaring Fork Motor Trail is a wonderful drive, offering four falls and Roaring Fork itself, which is one of the steepest gradients for water in the park. Cataract Falls near the Sugarlands Visitor Center is easily accessible.

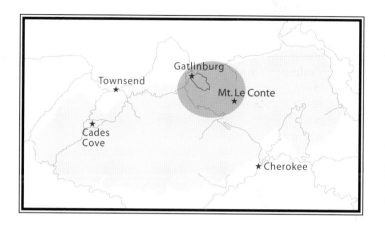

BASKINS CREEK FALLS

- **FALLS**
- **35 FOOT DROP**
- **3.2 MILE ROUNDTRIP MODERATE HIKE**

*N*ear a grassy open area where a pile of rocks marks an old house site, Falls Branch does a two step off a sandstone ledge. The first step is 20 feet to a 3 foot shelf with the second step another 15 feet to the rocky bottom. This beautiful falls gets little publicity, so the trail is not heavily traveled.

The falls begins when 5 foot wide Falls Branch falls onto a ledge which funnels the water through a 2 foot opening. The

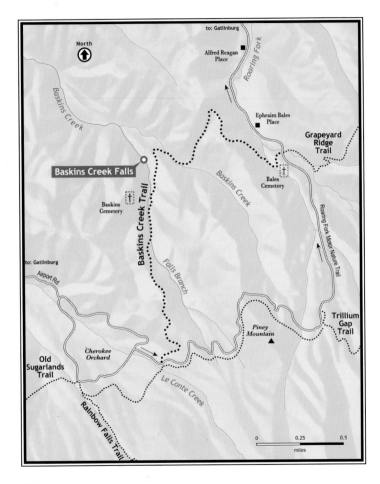

North

to: Gatlinburg

Alfred Reagan Place

Roaring Fork

Baskins Creek

Ephraim Bales Place

Grapeyard Ridge Trail

Baskins Creek Falls

Baskins Creek Trail

Baskins Creek

Baskins Cemetery

Bales Cemetery

Roaring Fork Motor Nature Trail

Falls Branch

to: Gatlinburg

Airport Rd.

Old Sugarlands Trail

Cherokee Orchard

Piney Mountain

Trillium Gap Trail

Le Conte Creek

Rainbow Falls Trail

0   0.25   0.5
miles

Baskins Creek Falls

creek runs off to the left with no pool at the base of the falls. One hundred fifty feet below the falls the creek tumbles another 6 feet to a small pool before rushing on toward downtown Gatlinburg where it passes in front of the elementary school.

The Roaring Fork Sandstone, which forms the cliff, exhibits several geological structures. To the left of the falls vertical fractures known as joints can be seen in the rock. A layering effect can be seen to the right of the waterfall.

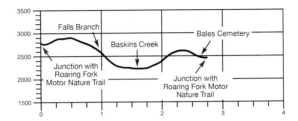

Observe the hemlock to the right of the falls' top which bends out over the cliff. Also to the right, about 100 feet, is a wet weather falls. We've noticed mud daubers' nests stuck to the side of the cliff. The mud is from the creek below.

The large boulder at the base of the falls may have fallen from the cliff at the spot where the falls now flow. The downed trees, rocks and boulders point to the ever changing effect of moving water shaping mountains and valleys.

Around mile 1.2 a side trail ascends the ridge to the small Baskins Cemetery. Most of the tombstones have no writing, but a few tell of deaths around the turn of the 20th century.

Baskins Creek gets its name from a man called Bearskin Joe who lived nearby and was noted for his prowess as a hunter, especially of bear. The creek was called Bearskin Joe's Creek which later became Bearskin Creek. This name was eventually misunderstood and shortened to Baskins Creek.

TO GET THERE: From Gatlinburg's main street (Highway 441) turn onto Historic Nature Trail-Airport Road at Light #8. At 2.6

miles from the light pass the Noah 'Bud' Ogle Nature Trail.
Beyond the Ogle Place where the road divides, take the right fork.
At 3.4 miles pass the Rainbow Falls–Bullhead trailheads which
lead to Mt. Le Conte. At 3.7 miles turn right onto the one-way
Roaring Fork Motor Nature Trail. Baskins Creek Trail starts 0.2
mile up the road on the left. Although Roaring Fork Motor Nature
Trail is closed in the winter, you can still park at a pullout near the
gate and walk up 0.2 mile to the start of Baskins Creek Trail.

Baskins Creek Trail weaves through an impressive forest of
chestnut oaks, red maples, Northern red oaks, Eastern hemlocks, striped maples and large blackgums. At 0.2 mile, you
climb an easy piney ridge with many trees killed by the native
Southern pine bark beetle.

Descending steeply from the ridge toward Falls Branch, you
pass through more pines and an abundance of mountain laurel. Cross Falls Branch on stepping stones at 1.0 mile. The trail
now descends more steeply, down a short canyon dug by the
rollicking branch. On the right, numerous handsome outcrops
of Roaring Fork Sandstone are visible. The rock is named for
the stream you'll hear roar near the end of this trail. Big blocks
of white vein quartz are often associated with this type of rock.

At 1.4 miles, an unmaintained side trail takes off to Baskins
Creek Falls. Although this spur receives plenty of use, it is
steep, slippery, and dangerous where it cuts down to the base
of the falls. If you don't feel you can make the descent safely,
don't even try it.

Back on Baskins Creek Trail, you can return to the trailhead

Cataract Falls

the way you came or continue along Baskins Creek Trail to the Bales Cemetery at the other end of Roaring Fork Motor Nature Trail. If you do the latter, it will be 2.7 miles back to your car via Baskins Creek Trail.

CATARACT FALLS
- **CASCADE**
- **40 FOOT DROP**
- **0.7 MILE ROUNDTRIP EASY WALK**

*C*ataract Falls is a narrow cascade that slides 40 feet down a rocky face before Cataract Branch joins Fighting Creek. Though small, Cataract is easily reached from the Sugarlands Visitor Center.

TO GET THERE: Begin at Sugarlands Visitor Center. Go out the front door, turn right and walk under the breezeway past the restrooms. Take Fighting Creek Nature Trail and cross the creek

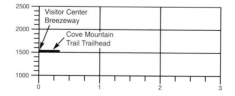

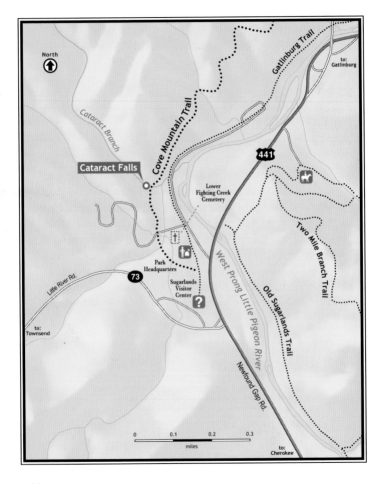

North

Cataract Branch

Cove Mountain Trail

Gatlinburg Trail

to: Gatlinburg

441

Cataract Falls

Lower Fighting Creek Cemetery

Two Mile Branch Trail

Park Headquarters

Sugarlands Visitor Center

West Prong Little Pigeon River

Old Sugarlands Trail

73

Little River Rd.

to: Townsend

Newfound Gap Rd.

to: Cherokee

| 0 | 0.1 | 0.2 | 0.3 |

miles

on a bridge. The trail to Cataract Falls forks to the right just after the bridge. Follow the trail 0.2 mile to the falls.

FERN BRANCH FALLS
- **CASCADE**
- **45 FOOT DROP**
- **3.6 MILE ROUNDTRIP MODERATE HIKE**

$\mathcal{F}$ern Branch Falls is a small cascade on the east side of Porters Creek which slips 45 feet over a rock face of Thunderhead Sandstone. Though not always a spectacular sight, Fern Branch Falls is a pleasant stopping point on the way up Porters Creek. Water from the small Fern Branch slides down the exposed rock. After a couple of small steps of 3-4 feet the cascade goes two-thirds of the way to a shelf.

The water then slides to the base over bare stone into rocks and downed trees which litter the base. Wildflowers

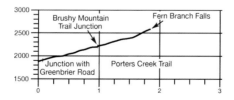

Fern Branch Falls

bloom in abundance in the moist area below the falls. Trillium and white phacelia are especially plentiful. The abundant ferns leave no doubt as to the naming of this branch. Over 65 species of ferns and fern allies thrive in the park.

TO GET THERE: The Porters Creek trailhead is in the Greenbrier section of the park. Turn off Highway 321 about 6 miles east of Gatlinburg. Pass the Greenbrier Ranger Station and continue up the gravel road. The trailhead is 4 miles from the highway.

It's a 1.8 mile moderate walk on the Porters Creek Trail to reach Fern Branch. The falls are to the left of the trail 0.4 mile after crossing Porters Creek on a footlog. Take advantage of the walk to see some of the Smokies long history. The first mile of the walk is on a wide, well maintained road. Rock walls built by those who lived and farmed the area wind through the woods. They still stand, but no longer separate fields or contain livestock.

A small cemetery lies up stone steps 30 yards beyond the first bridge. Original white settlers and their grandchildren, who died young, are resting in this secluded spot. David Profitt, a Civil War veteran, lies with Whaleys, Ownbys, and Profitts. Most of the dates range from 1900 to 1910.

The cabin at the end of the road on the right was built by the Smoky Mountain Hiking Club in the 1930s. The club built the structure of logs from two cabins on the Whaley homestead. The buildings are now owned and maintained by the park service.

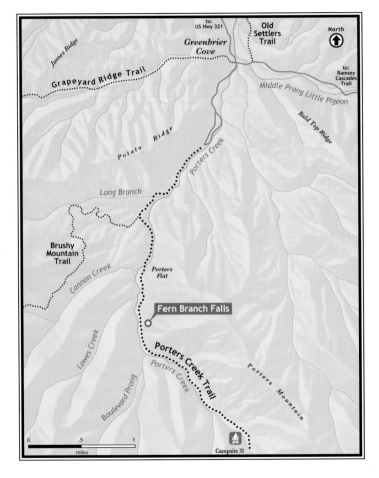

The entire walk is very pleasant because it follows Porters Creek, which begins on the side of Mt. Le Conte. The drive to the trailhead parallels the Little Pigeon River which has many small falls and cascades.

GROTTO FALLS

- **FALLS**
- **25 FOOT DROP**
- **2.6 MILE ROUNDTRIP MODERATE HIKE**

$\mathcal{G}$rotto Falls is named for the cave-like appearance of the rocks behind the falls. The water of Roaring Fork free-falls 18 feet after a short 7 foot cascade at the top. The falls spread to a 12 foot width from its 2 foot beginning in the sandstone above. It's fun to walk on the trail behind the waterfall and is the easiest way to get to the other side.

The 20 by 30 foot pool at the base of the falls is a favorite

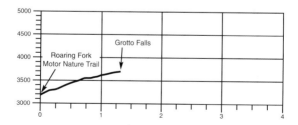

Grotto Falls (and team of llamas bound for Mt. Le Conte Lodge)

spot to cool hot feet. In its chilly waters many salamanders can be found. Some 30 species of salamanders live in the Smokies. More varieties of salamanders live in the park than in any other area of comparable size in the world.

Roaring Fork is said to be one of the steepest creeks in the eastern United States. It loses 1 mile in elevation from its source near the top of Mt. Le Conte to its mouth in Gatlinburg. A 6 foot cascade spills from the pool at Grotto's base. A double falls (4 and 12 feet) with a deep clear green pool is 100 yards below Grotto.

Notice the difference in the rocks around the falls. The dark shale below the falls is softer and thus more easily worn than the harder sandstone above and behind the falls. At Grotto, Thunderhead Sandstone is the more resistant rock above the falls with a silty layer of Elkmont Sandstone below. The Greenbrier Fault is on the trail to the falls.

The Grotto Falls Trail is a good complement to the Roaring Fork Motor Nature Trail with its scenic views and historic buildings. A full day could include Rainbow and Grotto falls and Place of a Thousand Drips.

TO GET THERE: From Gatlinburg's main street (Highway 441) turn onto Historic Nature Trail-Airport Road at Light #8. At 2.6 miles from the light pass the Noah 'Bud' Ogle log home. At 3.4 miles, pass the Rainbow Falls–Bullhead trailheads which lead to Mt. Le Conte. At 3.7 miles turn right onto the one-way Roaring Fork Motor Nature Trail (booklet at the gate). Note:

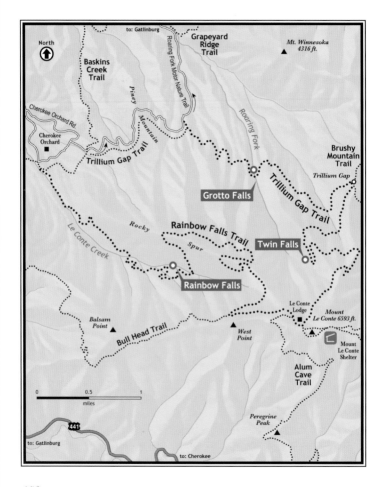

North

to: Gatlinburg

Grapeyard Ridge Trail

Mt. Winnesoka 4316 ft.

Baskins Creek Trail

Roaring Fork Motor Nature Trail

Piney Mountain

Cherokee Orchard Rd.

Cherokee Orchard

Trillium Gap Trail

Roaring Fork

Brushy Mountain Trail

Trillium Gap

Trillium Gap Trail

Grotto Falls

Rocky

Rainbow Falls Trail

Twin Falls

Spur

Le Conte Creek

Rainbow Falls

Le Conte Lodge

Mount Le Conte 6593 ft.

Balsam Point

Bull Head Trail

West Point

Mount Le Conte Shelter

Alum Cave Trail

0   0.5   1
miles

Peregrine Peak

441

to: Gatlinburg

to: Cherokee

The Roaring Fork Motor Nature Trail is closed in the winter. Two miles from the gate (5.7 miles from Gatlinburg) the Grotto Falls Trail begins on the right beyond a parking area.

The trail begins in a mature hemlock forest which gives way to tuliptree and yellow buckeye. Small streams have to be crossed, but pose no problem except in the rainiest seasons.

Trillium, violets, and spring-beauty flourish in late April and early May. Grotto Falls is 1.3 miles from the parking area. Trillium Gap is 1.7 miles beyond the falls. From the gap, it's an easy walk to Brushy Mountain, a heath bald with beautiful views of Greenbrier, Mt. Le Conte, and Pigeon Forge. It's 3.6 miles from Trillium Gap to the top of Mt. Le Conte.

HUSKEY BRANCH FALLS
- **CASCADE**
- **50 FOOT DROP, 120 FOOT RUN**
- **4.3 MILE ROUNDTRIP MODERATE WALK**

*H*uskey Branch is a pleasant stream that slides down bare metasandstone into the Little River. The cascade begins as an 8 foot falls before traveling 110 feet to the river. Although not as steep as many other cascades in the Smokies, it has a beauty of its own, especially when the rhododendron are in bloom.

Notice the shaley siltstone of Elkmont Sandstone at the top left of the falls which is more easily worn than the fine-grained, quartz-streaked Thunderhead Sandstone. The stream flows through a crack formed by a fault line that is associated with the Oconaluftee Fault which runs along the Cucumber Gap Trail just uphill from the cascade. The cascade starts its journey to the river through the channel once occupied by the siltstone.

The Huskey name is associated with this area of the Smokies because several Huskey families lived in Sugarlands. All were descendants of James Wesley Huskey who was one of the original settlers of the Smokies in the 1800s. Sam Huskey had a store in the Sugarlands.

Sit on the bench to enjoy a picnic or the sound of the water. The cascade passes under a bridge on Little River Trail. A large, deep pool in the Little River is at the base of the cascade—look for rainbow trout facing upstream. The Little River splashes and tumbles over many rocks and boulders as

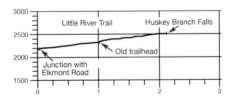

Huskey Branch Falls

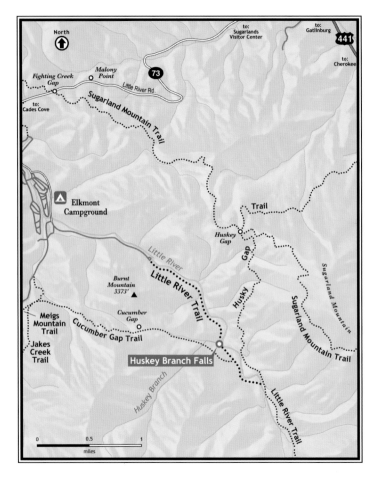

it falls from its headwaters high up the sides of Clingmans Dome, the highest peak in the Smokies.

TO GET THERE: Travel the Little River Road for 5 miles from Sugarlands Visitor Center toward Cades Cove. Turn into the Elkmont area, then turn left just before entering the campground. Continue on to the Little River trailhead that is located at a gated road on the left.

Little River Trail is a moderate walk that parallels the river on an old roadbed. Icicles cling to the rocky cliffs in the winter. Wildflowers abound in the spring and summer. Fall's show of color is particularly pretty in this hardwood forest. The cascade runs right beside and under the trail, 2.1 miles from the trailhead.

Jakes Creek Falls

JAKES CREEK FALLS

- **WATERFALL**
- **6 FOOT DROP**
- **2.4 MILE ROUNDTRIP MODERATE HIKE**

This small waterfall on Jakes Creek flows amid large boulders a short distance below the junctions of Cherry Branch, Waterdog Branch, and Newt Prong. The stream cascades approximately 100 feet, then splits into two streams to fall 6 feet over Thunderhead Sandstone boulders into a large plunge pool. The pool is 30 feet across and about 8-10 feet deep. Maple, tuliptree, hemlock, buckeye, and rhododendron surround this cool spot just off the trail. A piece of steel cable, a remnant of logging days in the early 1900s, lays beside the small side trail leading down to the plunge pool. Numerous cascades punctuate Jakes Creek between Elkmont and the footlog at Waterdog Branch.

TO GET THERE: Travel the Little River Road 5 miles from Sugarlands Visitor Center toward Townsend. Turn into the Elkmont area and take a left just before the campground. Continue through the historic Elkmont community. Stop at the top of the hill at the Jakes Creek trailhead.

The Jakes Creek Trail climbs along an old railroad bed through a hardwood forest that has plenty of wildflowers in the spring. Pass the Cucumber Gap Trail on the left at 0.3 mile and the Meigs Mountain Trail on the right at 0.4 miles. Large

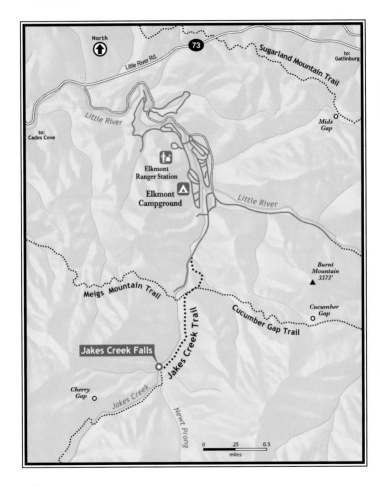

North

73

Little River Rd.

Sugarland Mountain Trail

to: Gatlinburg

Little River

Mids Gap

to: Cades Cove

Elkmont Ranger Station

Elkmont Campground

Little River

Burnt Mountain 3373'

Meigs Mountain Trail

Cucumber Gap Trail

Cucumber Gap

Jakes Creek Trail

Jakes Creek Falls

Jakes Creek

Cherry Gap

Newt Prong

0   .25   0.5
miles

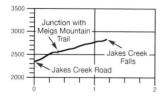

rock outcroppings of fine-grained Thunderhead Sandstone are on the left at various places along the trail. Jakes Creek tumbles and falls far below on the right. The small waterfall is a wonderful cool spot on the right at 1.2 miles, just before reaching the footlog over Waterdog Branch.

LAUREL FALLS

- **CASCADE**
- **85 FOOT DROP, 90 FOOT RUN**
- **2.5 MILE ROUNDTRIP MODERATE WALK**

*L*aurel Falls is a heavily visited falls. It is unusual in that the trail divides the falls into two nearly equal parts. Laurel Branch begins high atop Cove Mountain and flows through virgin forest before arriving at the sandstone ledges of Thunderhead Formation to stairstep its way toward the Little River.

Laurel Branch slides 20 feet before it scatters across the rocky cliff face to fall 30 feet more. The first ledge is 14 feet wide and tilted 30° to the right. The water falls another 16 feet to the trail ledge which is 38 feet from front to back and 45 feet across. A partial bridge has been strategically placed for easy crossing of the creek. This is a favorite resting spot for hikers. The boulders around the pool and several pockets in the smooth sandstone are perfect for cooling hot feet in the summer.

The creek falls off the ledge over which the trail passes 22 feet to another ledge (10 foot). The water slips to the right to form a 12 foot wide stream which drops another 12 feet to a last ledge. The final 5 foot fall ends in a pool. The section of the falls below the trail rivals that above. Enjoy the entire display.

Early settlers called rhododendron 'laurel'. It's no mystery why this area was known as Laurel Branch and Falls. This lovely spot is very popular and often crowded. Try to catch it in the off-season or in the early morning or evening.

TO GET THERE: The trailhead is at Fighting Creek Gap on Little River Road. It's 3.8 miles west of Sugarlands Visitor Center and

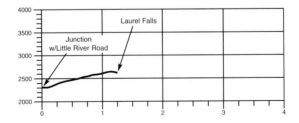

Laurel Falls

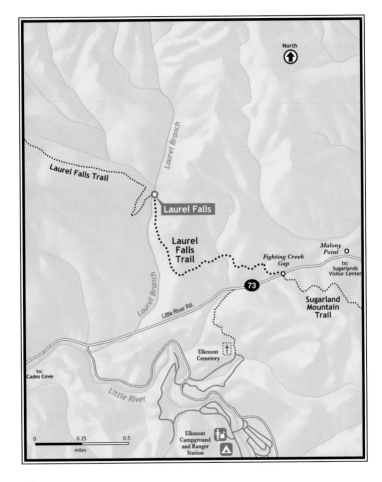

14 miles east of Townsend. Parking is available on both sides of the road. The 1.3 mile paved trail to Laurel Falls is a self-guided nature trail. A leaflet describing noteworthy trail features can be obtained for a small charge at the trailhead.

The trail climbs through oak and hemlock with views of Meigs and Blanket mountains to the southwest. In mid-May the mountain laurel blooms abundantly in a wonderful show of white and pink. Steep cliffs of Thunderhead Sandstone are reached before the falls. Return to the parking area by the same route.

A longer walk to the Cove Mountain firetower (no longer open to the public) can be made by continuing 2.9 miles on the trail beyond the falls. The trail passes through beautiful old-growth forest. Allow plenty of time for this 8 mile roundtrip hike.

MANNIS BRANCH FALLS

- **FALLS**
- **40 FOOT DROP**
- **ROADSIDE**

*M*annis Branch Falls is a roadside waterfall that is best seen in the winter and early spring when there are no leaves on the trees. It provides a nice show in summer, but requires a walk down to Little River. Mannis Branch runs through a 3 foot opening of Elkmont Sandstone to fall 30 feet to a small shelf with a shallow plunge pool. The creek then drops 10 more feet in a small cascade. Even though the falls is only 3 feet wide, it quickly spreads to over 60 feet by the time it reaches the base. Several large (10-12 foot) streaks of quartz in the stone can be seen in the water between the second smaller cascade and the cascade into the river. The stream flows 75 yards over large rocks to another small cascade to fall into the Little River.

Mannis Branch Falls

This falls is on a fault line that is a branch of the Oconaluftee Fault running across the Smokies from the North Carolina side into Tennessee. The Oconaluftee Fault is one of the major faults that formed the Great Smokies.

Due to dense vegetation along the road and at its base, Mannis Branch Falls can be difficult to see. However, after a good rain it is one of the more beautiful falls in the Smokies.

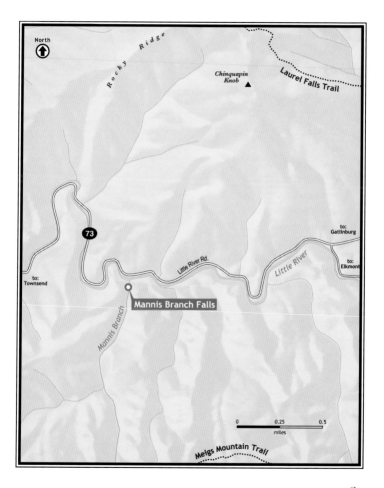

North

Rocky Ridge

Chinquapin Knob

Laurel Falls Trail

73

to: Gatlinburg

Little River Rd.

Little River

to: Elkmont

to: Townsend

Mannis Branch

Mannis Branch Falls

0   0.25   0.5
miles

Meigs Mountain Trail

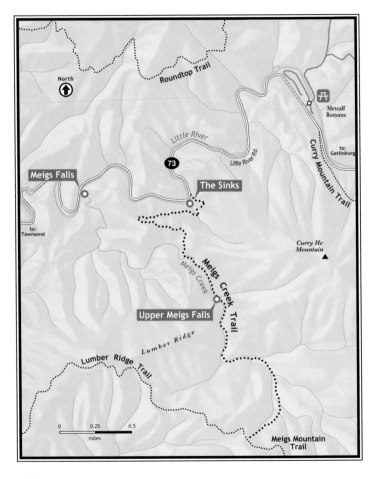

TO GET THERE: Mannis Branch Falls is on the south side of Little River Road, 1.5 miles west of the road to Elkmont Campground between Gatlinburg and Townsend. There is a paved pulloff in a nearby curve. A small path 75 yards upstream from the parking area leads down to the river for a good view across to the falls. Do not attempt to cross Little River! The parking area is 3.4 miles east of Metcalf Bottoms Picnic Area and 11.2 miles east of the intersection at the Townsend "Y" on Little River Road. Use extreme caution when driving narrow, winding Little River Road. Do not stop or drive too slowly on the roadway. Use pullouts.

MEIGS FALLS

- **FALLS**
- **28 FOOT DROP**
- **ROADSIDE**

Several small tributaries converge on the northern slope of Meigs Mountain to form Meigs Creek, which flows through a gorge to reach the Little River at Highway 73 (Little River Road). The falls begin with two modest steps of 5 feet and 2 feet when Meigs Creek emerges from a tunnel of dense rhododendron, hardwoods, and pine. The creek travels 45 feet from the top steps to drop 5 feet into a 3 foot wide gutter which shifts the flow from right to left about 15 feet. The water then plunges 28 feet over exposed Thunderhead

Meigs Falls

Sandstone to form a beautiful sight which can be seen from the road.

The creek spreads from 12 to 16 feet until the water hits a ledge which further spreads the water to 30 feet. On this ledge the water shifts back to the right. The creek steps down a couple more ledges before going 125 feet to join the Little River.

Meigs Mountain, Creek, and Falls are named after Colonel Return Jonathan Meigs (1734-1823) who acted as U.S. agent to the Cherokee from 1801 to 1823. After serving with distinction in the Revolutionary War, Meigs moved to Ohio from his home in Connecticut. He was appointed as the Indian agent to assist in civilizing the Cherokee and to convince them to move west of the Mississippi River.

In 1802, Meigs surveyed the boundary of the land the Cherokee ceded to the settlers in a treaty. The line ran from the top of Chilhowee Mountain to the crest of the Smokies. It was difficult to sight the line due to the dense growth and steep ridges. At one point a large blanket was put on a pole so that it could be spotted. Meigs Mountain is north of Blanket Mountain along the surveyed line.

Meigs suggested that land be given to individual Cherokee and that each should be granted citizenship. The states reacted vehemently to this proposal which was before its time. Meigs' name on the map attests to Return Jonathan Meigs' service to Cherokee and settlers alike.

Near Meigs Falls was a swinging railroad bridge which

went from cliff top to near the Little River with no support underneath the bridge. This bridge was used in the early 1900s in the logging operations of the area.

TO GET THERE: Meigs Falls is on the south side of Little River Road 13 miles from Sugarlands Visitor Center and 5 miles from the intersection of Highway 73 (Little River Road) with the Laurel Creek Road near Townsend. The Sinks are about 1 mile east of Meigs Falls.

Enjoy Meigs Falls from the pulloff, which is a great vantage point for photographs. No trail goes to the falls.

PLACE OF A THOUSAND DRIPS
- **CASCADES**
- **80 FOOT DROP**
- **ROADSIDE**

*P*lace of a Thousand Drips is well named. Cliff Branch falls 80 feet through many routes before converging with Roaring Fork which rushes by on the opposite side of the road. The single stream spreads to 55 feet wide at the road. Although the water falls 80 feet it travels much farther over the slightly slanted (about 15°) Thunderhead Sandstone. Several streamlets fall 10 and 20 feet at a time.

Place of a Thousand Drips is a multi-faceted diamond with many surprises of light and water when viewed from

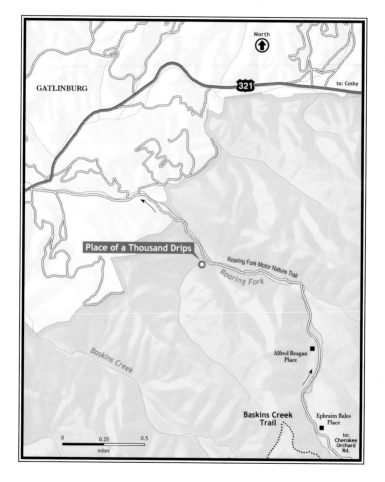

Place of a Thousand Drips

various angles. Walk around to fully enjoy this jewel of the Smokies. Thousands upon thousands of years from now a small canyon will be here, but for now the small trickles of water work away. The jumble of stones to the right of the falls is evidence of the changing nature of the area.

Ferns and moss make this a lush, green location. Hemlocks shade this area which is already cool due to evaporation. Sit on the small bench at the base of the massive sandstone cliff to listen to Roaring Fork and Thousand Drips.

TO GET THERE: A pulloff at 4.9 miles on the Roaring Fork Motor Nature Trail is the place to park. The auto tour is a 5.5 mile one lane, one way paved road beginning at the upper end of the Cherokee Orchard Road, 3.7 miles from traffic Light #8 in Gatlinburg. Another beautiful site is a 65 foot falls on the left at 4.8 miles. Parking is not readily available here. It's best to walk back from Thousand Drips. Note: Roaring Fork Motor Nature Trail is closed in winter.

RAINBOW FALLS
- **FALLS**
- **75 FOOT DROP**
- **5.5 MILE ROUNDTRIP MODERATE-DIFFICULT HIKE**

 ainbow Falls is one of the few actual falls in the park. Le Conte Creek free falls 75 feet from a double ledge of gray Thunderhead Sandstone to the rocks below. The water rushes quickly on down the mountainside in small cascades. The first cascade at the base of the falls is 8-10 feet.

Rainbow Falls is a tremendous sight in the wettest times of the year with the swollen creek pounding the rocks at the base. Normally the width of the stream is 6 feet at the top and 15 to 20 feet at the base. A footlog below the 75 foot falls provides a good view. The afternoon sun can produce a rainbow effect, thus the name.

In the winter, ice from the spray transforms the trail, rocks, and bridge into a beautiful but dangerous sight. Prolonged cold can cause ice to build up from the bottom and down from the top to form a column of ice. Although rare, it's most impressive.

It's a nice cool spot in the summer as a way station to Le Conte's summit. Spring's wildflowers are plentiful while fall presents a different spectrum of colors. Remember that water flow depends on rainfall, so it can be a trickle or a torrent. Many large hemlock and rhododendron thickets border the creek.

TO GET THERE: In downtown Gatlinburg, on Highway 441, turn onto Historic Nature Trail-Airport Road at Light #8. At 2.6 miles from the light pass the Noah 'Bud' Ogle Nature Trail. Beyond the Ogle Place where the road divides, take the right fork. At 3.4 miles park at the Rainbow Falls–Bullhead trails parking area. The multiple-use Rainbow Falls Trail goes 2.8 miles to Rainbow Falls on its way to the top of Mt. Le Conte

Rainbow Falls

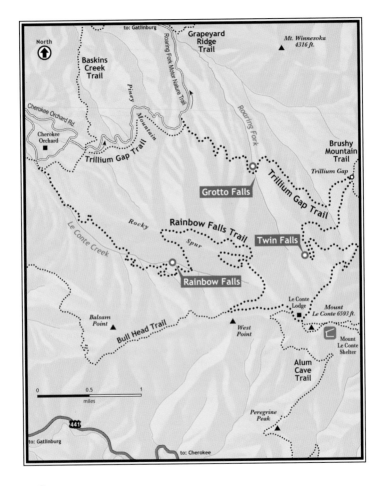

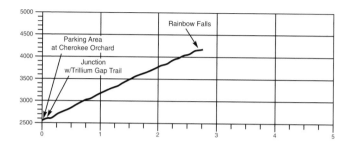

(6.7 miles). The trail follows Le Conte Creek up to the falls. One is never far from the sound of the mountain stream which falls from high up the slopes of Mt. Le Conte toward its union with the Little Pigeon River in Gatlinburg. This creek was once known as Mill Creek because it had 14 tub mills similar to the one at the Noah 'Bud' Ogle place. The remains of a cabin are beside the creek at about 0.25 mile from the beginning. This could have been the site of one of the many mills on the creek.

At a switchback is an overlook with views of Sevier County to the north. The first of two footlogs is crossed approximately half way up. About 0.3 mile from Rainbow Falls is an 8 foot waterfall on the right. The trail is heavily used and often crowded. Sometimes parking can be a problem. Get an early start to see this wonder.

Ramsey Cascades

RAMSEY CASCADES

- **CASCADE**
- **105 FOOT DROP, 122 FOOT RUN**
- **8 MILE ROUNDTRIP DIFFICULT HIKE**

*R*amsey Cascades is one of the most beautiful falls of water in the park. It's also one of the highest at 105 feet. The cascade provides the best show in the wetter seasons of winter and spring. However, since the headwaters of Ramsey Prong are high up on the sides of Mt. Guyot, the second highest peak in the park at 6,621 feet, any season has a good flow and thus is picturesque.

The water of Ramsey Prong falls over a jumble of Thunderhead Sandstone. This is the same type of boulder that litters the woods on the trail to Ramsey Cascades. Notice that the sandstone is inclined 30° away from an observer at the

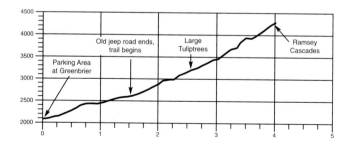

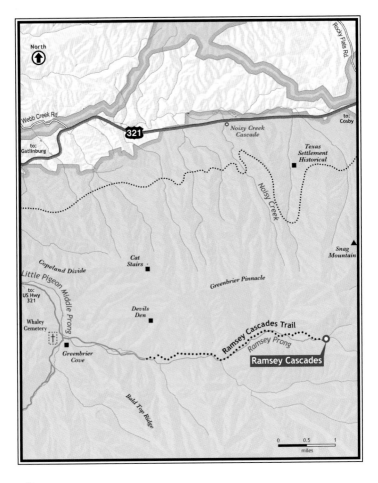

base. The constant flow has smoothed the rocks to rounded shapes. The boulders farther from the creek are more angular.

At the top of the cascades, Ramsey Prong is separated into two streams by large boulders with rhododendron growing on them. The stream on the left is the larger of the two. The water hits many outcroppings as it drops 85 feet to a 70 foot ledge with a 25 foot stream width. Several pools spread and redirect the stream's flow. Notice how the water has worn the surface of the sandstone to reveal a different underlying texture.

The water leaves the ledge in a 6 foot wide stream to slide under a large overhanging boulder. This 25 foot slide drops approximately 8 feet to where the water falls 12 feet into another pool. Rhododendron and hemlock form a green frame year round.

We've seen Ramsey Cascades completely frozen over in mid-February. The rocks were covered in ice and snow. Even though no moving water could be seen, it could be heard. One hundred feet below the falls is a scenic crossing of Ramsey Prong. Stop for good photos of the cascade.

The temptation to climb the rocks and boulders at the base and sides of the cascade is strong. This is VERY DANGEROUS! A number of people have been killed at this cascade over the years. Enjoy the view from the bottom, which is a good spot for a picnic.

Ramsey Cascades and Prong are named for the Ramsey family who lived on Webb Creek and had a hunting cabin on this stream. Over the years the creek and cascade took the name from the people who roamed this area in search of game.

TO GET THERE: From Gatlinburg go east on Highway 321 toward Cosby. Turn at the Greenbrier sign which is 6 miles from Traffic light #3 at the intersection of Highways 321 and 441 in Gatlinburg. Follow the Middle Prong of the Little Pigeon River for 3.2 miles. Make a left turn over the wooden bridge. The road dead ends at the trailhead 1.5 miles from the turn.

After the parking area, the trail turns left and crosses a wooden footbridge. The trail passes through several boulder fields which were probably formed 10,000 to 12,000 years ago. The trail crosses Ramsey Branch on another footbridge. At 1.5 miles the old gravel road ends in a loop.

Continue straight ahead on the foot trail which climbs gradually through rhododendron, large hemlocks and tuliptrees. At 2.1 miles the trail descends to a foot log, then turns left through some large trees. This virgin forest contains silverbell, sweet birch, and enormous tuliptrees. The trail levels off for 0.25 mile before climbing again. At 2.7 miles is an easy access to the creek which is a good spot to rest before ascending again.

At 3.9 miles, after another foot log, the trail occasionally climbs rock steps as the cascade is approached. Take extra care when crossing the stream because wet rocks can be slippery and unsteady. Return to the parking area by the same route.

The hike to Ramsey Cascades is a full day's walk, but worth the time and effort.

The Sinks

THE SINKS

- **CASCADE**
- **12 FOOT DROP**
- **ROADSIDE**

*T*he Little River sinks suddenly and dramatically over tilted formations of Thunderhead Sandstone. The river is 70 feet wide with a large flow of water. The cascade

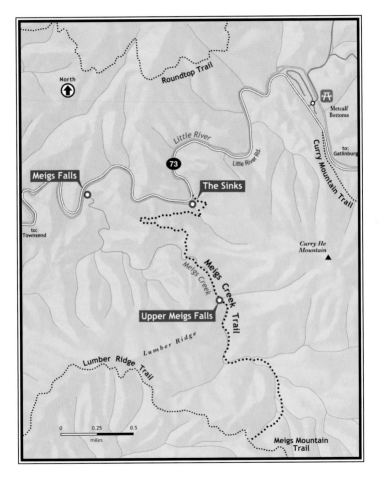

North

Roundtop Trail

Metcalf
Bottoms

Little River

73

Little River Rd.

Curry Mountain Trail

to:
Gatlinburg

Meigs Falls

The Sinks

to:
Townsend

Curry He
Mountain

Meigs Creek

Meigs Creek Trail

Upper Meigs Falls

Lumber Ridge

Lumber Ridge Trail

0   0.25   0.5
miles

Meigs Mountain
Trail

more than makes up in volume for what it lacks in height. A large, deep plunge pool at the base of The Sinks is a beautiful sight any time of the year.

Highway 73 (Little River Road) follows the railroad bed of the Little River Railroad from Townsend to Elkmont. The Little River Lumber Company constructed the railway to haul lumber from its vast operation in the Smokies. In addition to hauling cut trees from the Smokies' virgin forest, it carried visitors on excursion and 'mixed' (that is, tourists and lumber) runs. Daily service from Knoxville to Elkmont was begun in 1909 and continued until 1925 when the line closed. The cut through the rocks near The Sinks was originally for the railroad.

TO GET THERE: The Sinks is below a bridge between Gatlinburg and Townsend on Highway 73 (Little River Road) 12 miles from the Sugarlands Visitor Center and 6 miles from the intersection of Highway 73 with the Laurel Creek Road at the Townsend "Y".

TWIN FALLS
- **CASCADE**
- **300+ FEET**
- **9 MILE ROUNDTRIP STRENUOUS HIKE**

Two small streams tumble down the steep upper slopes of Mt. Le Conte, the Smokies' third highest peak. Trillium Gap trail provides a good view of these narrow lacy twin cascades on the side of the mountain. They are the uppermost headwaters of Roaring Fork Creek, said to be the steepest stream in the park. In its descent from Le Conte's summit to its mouth on the West Prong of the Little Pigeon River it loses 1 mile in elevation. Floods along this drainage are a sight to behold.

The two falls can be seen from the trail only in months with no leaf cover. In the summer, only one part of Twin Falls is visible from the trail because of the thick vegetation. However, a closer look at the left of the twins is available at a switchback on the Trillium Gap Trail at 5,200 feet above sea level. The cascade is similar to Flat Creek Falls on the North Carolina side of the park. The exact length and height of these cascades are difficult to determine due to the terrain and vegetation. Beech trees, witch hobble, red spruce, and Fraser firs are in this northern hardwood forest. The rocks in the stream are of Thunderhead Sandstone.

There are many waterfalls and cascades along the 6.5 mile

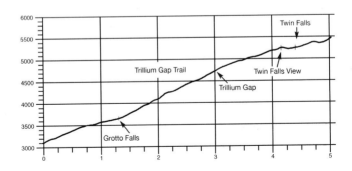

Twin Falls

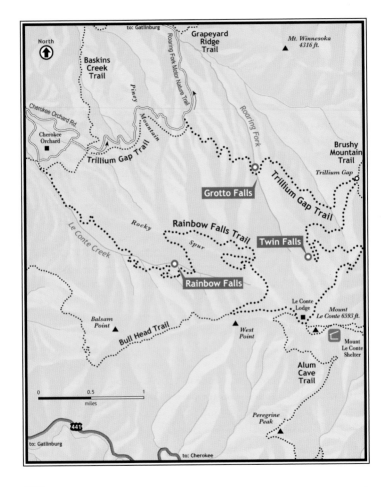

to: Gatlinburg

North

Grapeyard Ridge Trail

Mt. Winnesoka 4316 ft.

Baskins Creek Trail

Roaring Fork Motor Nature Trail

Piney Mountain

Cherokee Orchard Rd.

Cherokee Orchard

Roaring Fork

Brushy Mountain Trail

Trillium Gap

Trillium Gap Trail

Grotto Falls

Trillium Gap Trail

Le Conte Creek

Rocky

Rainbow Falls Trail

Spur

Twin Falls

Rainbow Falls

Le Conte Lodge

Mount Le Conte 6593 ft.

Balsam Point

Bull Head Trail

West Point

Mount Le Conte Shelter

Alum Cave Trail

0   0.5   1
miles

Peregrine Peak

441

to: Gatlinburg

to: Cherokee

length of Trillium Gap Trail. Twin Falls and Grotto Falls are the only ones accessible from trails. Others can be seen from the Roaring Fork Motor Nature Trail.

TO GET THERE: From Gatlinburg's main street (Highway 441), turn onto Historic Nature Trail-Airport Road at Light #8. At 2.6 miles from the light, pass the Noah 'Bud' Ogle Cabin and Nature Trail. Beyond the Ogle Place where the road divides, take the right fork. At 3.4 miles pass the Rainbow Falls-Bull-head trailheads. At 3.7 miles turn right onto the one-way Roaring Fork Motor Nature Trail (booklet at gate). Note: Roaring Fork Motor Nature Trail is closed in winter. Two miles from the gate (5.7 miles from the light in Gatlinburg) the Trillium Gap Trail to Grotto Falls begins on the right beyond a parking area.

It is 1.3 miles to Grotto Falls. The trail goes behind the falls and continues to Trillium Gap. At the trail intersection, the Trillium Gap Trail turns to the right to ascend Mt. Le Conte. The left trail is to Brushy Mountain with views of the Smokies and the Tennessee Valley. The trail that goes straight descends to Porters Creek in the Greenbrier area of the park.

Ascend the Trillium Gap Trail for a good view of Twin Falls at 1.2 miles from Trillium Gap (4.2 miles from the trailhead). The trail reaches the side of one of the twins at 1.5 miles from the gap and 4.5 miles from the parking area. This falls is best viewed on a trip to the summit of Mt. Le Conte, 2.0 miles beyond the cascade. Return to your car by the same route.

UPPER MEIGS FALLS

- **WATERFALL**
- **25 FOOT DROP**
- **3.6 MILES ROUNDTRIP MODERATE HIKE**

*U*pper Meigs Falls is a slightly smaller version of its downstream sibling, Meigs Falls, which can be seen from Little River Road. This upper falls is located along the Greenbrier Fault line which is one of the major geological faults in the formation of the Smokies. The small rock escarpment is made of the fine-grained, gray Thunderhead Sandstone, while the rock downstream is the softer Metcalf Phyllite. When Meigs Creek flows over the right side of the ledge, it is about 10 feet wide. In high water, the creek flows over the entire rock face. This is a beautiful spot surrounded by rosebay rhododendron, doghobble, maples, and yellow birch. A small plunge pool at the base of the falls is a nice spot to take pictures or have a picnic.

TO GET THERE: This hike on Meigs Creek Trail begins at The Sinks parking area 12 miles west of Sugarlands Visitor Center

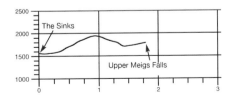

Upper Meigs Falls

on Little River Road. The trail moves up and away from the Little River and the sound of water. The trail then climbs a small ridge and descends to the first crossing of Meigs Creek. This is the first of four rock hop crossings of the creek. At 1.8 miles there is a small side trail on the right that leads to the base of Upper Meigs Falls. Return to the parking area by the same route.

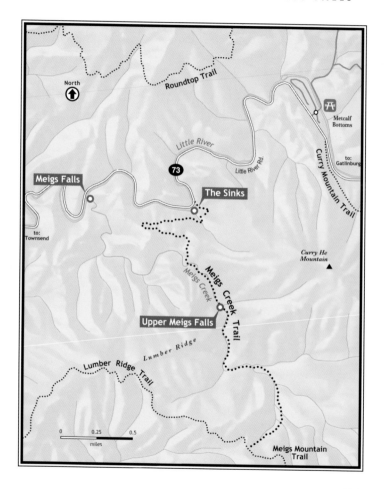

North

Roundtop Trail

Little River

73

Little River Rd.

Meigs Falls

The Sinks

to:
Townsend

Metcalf
Bottoms

to:
Gatlinburg

Curry Mountain Trail

Curry He
Mountain

Meigs Creek

Meigs Creek Trail

Upper Meigs Falls

Lumber Ridge

Lumber Ridge Trail

Meigs Mountain
Trail

0   0.25   0.5
miles

TIPS FOR WATERFALL PHOTOGRAPHY
by Kendall Chiles

EXPOSURE

Determining the correct exposure when photographing water scenes can be challenging as waterfalls and cascades appear white and streams are usually dark brown or green. This contrast in light and dark colors can fool your camera's light meter and give an incorrect exposure. Many of today's cameras can compensate for this situation to some degree. The best way to ensure a properly exposed photo is to take several photos at different exposures. This is a technique that is called bracketing. When using a film camera, this technique requires using a little more film, but it improves your chances of getting a good photograph. Digital camera users can easily delete undesirable photos. If you prefer your water photos to have the silky look, then you should use shutter speeds of 1/8 second to 2 seconds. Shutter speeds longer than 2 seconds can cause the waterfall to wash out and lose detail.

LIGHTING

The best lighting condition for waterfall and stream photography is overcast light. This type of lighting produces an evenly illuminated photograph with a lot of detail. Photographing water scenes in bright sun creates a high contrast image that has far less detail. Photographing in the early morning or late afternoon or evening can also produce good photographs similar to overcast situations.

TRIPODS

A tripod can be the most important piece of accessory equipment for nature photography. Using a tripod helps ensure that your photographs will be sharp and allows for the use of slower shutter speeds as mentioned above. Tripods can also force you to slow down and compose better photographs instead of just taking snapshots.

LENSES

Lens selection depends on how you want to compose the photo, your proximity to the scene, and the overall size of the scene. Zoom lenses are very useful for waterfall photography as you can alter your composition without changing lenses. A polarizing filter should be used on every waterfall/stream photo to help minimize glare that is virtually always present on water.

FILM/ISO SETTING

If you are still using film I would recommend using slow slide films due to their fine grain and excellent color reproduction. Fujichrome Velvia 50 has been the industry standard in nature photography since it was introduced in 1990. Fujichrome Velvia 100F and Fujichrome Provia 100F are also excellent slow speed films for nature photography. If you are using digital, then I would recommend setting your ISO to 100. This will give you the most detail and sharpness. I would only use a faster setting than 100 if the light was extremely low and I could not wait for the conditions to improve.

RESOURCES

Most of the following resources are available at the visitor centers in Great Smoky Mountains National Park. They may also be ordered by calling 1-888-898-9102 x26 or by visiting SmokiesStore.org

Smokies Guide The official newspaper of Great Smoky Mountains National Park.

Smokies Road Guide by Jerry DeLaughter. A complete guide to the roads of Great Smoky Mountains National Park. This is the only official guide to the main roads and gravel backroads of the park.

History Hikes of the Smokies by Michal Strutin. An in-depth guide to the 20 most culturally rich trails in the park. Includes many historic photos.

Hiking Map and Guide to Great Smoky Mountains National Park from the Earthwalk Press. One of the most up-to-date maps with extensive notes on trails and the park.

Hiking Trails of the Smokies by Great Smoky Mountains Association. The "brown book" or "hiker's bible." Provides in-depth narratives for all park trails.

Wildflowers of the Smokies by Peter White. A handy, pocket-sized field guide organized by flower color.

Day Hikes of the Smokies by Carson Brewer and friends. One of the better hiking guides available.

GSMNP: The Range of Life by Rose Houk. Brilliant photography and authoritative text provide an overview of the Smokies.

Great Smoky Mountains Wildflowers by Carlos Campbell, William F. Hutson, & Aaron J. Sharp. U.T. Press. An easy to carry pictorial guide to many common wildflowers.

Strangers in High Places by Michael Frome. A good history of the Great Smoky Mountains.

Our Southern Highlanders by Horace Kephart. A classic written in the early 1900s by one who worked to establish the park.

The Cades Cove Story by Randolph Shields. A short history of the white settlement in Cades Cove.

The Cherokees by Grace Steele Woodward. A good history of the Cherokee.

Exploring the Smokies by Rose Houk. Things to see and do in the Great Smoky Mountains.

INDEX OF WATERFALLS, STREAMS & TRAILS

Abrams Falls xvi, 35, 37, 39

Appalachian Trail 20, 54, 90, 100, 124, 128

Arbutus Branch 38

Baskins Creek 140

Baskins Creek Falls 137-143

Bearskin Creek 140

Big Creek 19, 20, 21, 26, 27, 30

Big Creek Trail 26, 29, 32

Bradley Fork Trail 69

Cataract Falls 136, 142-145

Chasteen Creek Falls 67-69

Chasteen Creek Trail 69

Cherry Branch 159

Cliff Branch 172

Clingmans Dome 100, 101, 102, 128, 157

Crooked Arm Cascade 40-43

Crooked Arm Creek 40, 43

Crooked Arm Ridge Trail 42, 43

Crying Creek 116

Cucumber Gap Trail 154, 159

Deep Creek 64, 65, 75, 79, 92, 95, 98

Deep Creek Trail 75, 79, 83, 94, 95, 98

Deeplow Gap Trail 83

Falls Branch 137, 141

Fern Branch Falls 145-149

Fighting Creek 143

Fighting Creek Nature Trail 143

Flat Creek Falls 69-72, 188

Flat Creek Trail 69

Forney Creek Cascade 100-105

Forney Creek Trail 102

Forney Ridge Trail 102, 128

Gabes Mountain Trail 115, 116

Greenbrier Ridge Trail 54

Grotto Falls xii, xiv, 149-153, 191

Grotto Falls Trail 151, 153

Gunter Fork xii, 21-26

Gunter Fork Trail 23, 26

Hammer Branch 94

Hazel Creek 124, 127, 128, 133

Hazel Creek Cascades 124-131

Hazel Creek Trail 125, 127, 131

Hen Wallow Creek 115

Hen Wallow Falls 115-119

Huskey Branch Falls 153-157

Indian Creek Falls 72-75, 76, 79, 83, 94, 98

Indian Creek Trail 75, 83, 94, 98

Indian Flats Falls 43-47

Indian Flats Prong 43, 47

Jakes Creek 159, 161

Jakes Creek Falls 158-161

Jakes Creek Trail 159

Juney Whank Falls xii, 75-79, 92, 98

Kephart Prong Trail 88

Laurel Creek 49, 51

Laurel Creek Cascade 48-51

Laurel Falls xii, 161-165

Le Conte Creek 175, 176

Little Creek Falls 79-83

Little River 34, 47, 53, 54, 56, 58, 153, 154, 157, 159, 161, 162, 165, 166, 169, 171, 172, 185, 187, 192, 194

Little River Trail 154, 157

Lumber Ridge Trail 58

Lynn Camp Prong 47, 51, 54

Lynn Camp Prong Cascades 47, 51-54

Mannis Branch 165

Mannis Branch Falls 165-169

Meigs Creek 169, 192, 194

Meigs Creek Trail 192

Meigs Falls 169-172, 192

Meigs Mountain Trail 159

Middle Prong Trail 47, 52, 54

Midnight Hole 26, 27-29, 32

Mill Creek 179

Mingo Creek 83

Mingo Falls 83-87

Moore Springs Branch 131, 132

Mouse Creek Falls 26, 29, 30-32

Mt. Le Conte 136, 141, 149, 150, 151, 153, 176, 179, 187, 191

Newt Prong 159

Noisy Creek Cascades 119-121

Panther Creek Trail 47

Place of a Thousand Drips 151, 172-175

Porters Creek 145, 147, 149, 191

Porters Creek Trail 147
Rainbow Falls 151, 176-179
Rainbow Falls Trail 176
Ramsey Cascades 180-184
Ramsey Prong 181, 183
Road Prong Cascade 105-108
Road Prong Falls 108,
  109-111
Road Prong Trail 106, 111
Roaring Fork xiv, 136, 149,
  151, 172, 175, 188
Rock Creek 116
Spruce Flats Creek 56
Spruce Flats Falls 35, 54-58
Stony Branch 38
Sweat Heifer Cascades 87-92
Sweat Heifer Creek 88, 90, 92
Sweat Heifer Trail 87
Talking Falls 109
The Sinks 172, 185-187, 192
Three Waterfalls Loop 92-93
Tom Branch Falls 75, 79, 83,
  95-98
Trickling Falls 105
Trillium Gap Trail 136, 153,
  187, 188, 191-203
Twentymile Cascade 131-133
Twentymile Creek 131, 133

Twin Falls 187-191
Upper Meigs Falls 192-195
Walker Camp Prong 106
Waterdog Branch 159, 161
Welch Ridge Trail 124, 128
White Oak Flats Branch 59,
  60
White Oak Flats Cascades
  59-61
Wilson Creek 38, 39
Wolf Ridge Trail 133

PHOTOGRAPHY CREDITS

Front and Back covers: Adam Jones

Kevin Adams: p. i, 46, 82, 86, 104, 146, 150

Kent Cave: p. 166

Kendall Chiles: p. 29, 48, 170

Liz Domingue: p. 55, 111, 155, 189

Hal Hubbs: p. iii, 22, 158

Adam Jones: p. 74, 96, 177, 180, 185

Byron Jorjorian: p. 117, 146

Mary Ann Kressig: p. 142

Bill Lea: p. 39

Charles Maynard: p. 91

David Morris: p. 42, 59, 68, 71, 78, 108, 121, 127, 132, 139, 174, 193

Nye Simmons: p.53

Jerry Whaley: p. 31, 163

ABOUT THE AUTHORS

Hal Hubbs, at home in Seymour, Tennessee, enjoys hiking, photography, and most any outdoor activities. Hal and his wife Elizabeth have a son, Will.

Charles Maynard is an author, storyteller, and United Methodist minister. He combines his love of hiking, waterfalls, and the mountains as often as possible. He and his wife Janice live in Northeast Tennessee and enjoy the outdoors with their daughters, Caroline and Anna, and their families.

David Morris takes time off from his career as a nurse anesthetist to hike and enjoy photography in the mountains. He and his wife Carol live in Seymour, Tennessee. They are both park volunteers and occasionally hike with their six sons and their families.